This teaching radically transforⁱ
be in God. When I first heard it,
weapons needed to take by my life from the influence of fear. Since then
my life has been full of freedom to be bold in Christ. My voice and its
value have been restored. I have been able to do things for Christ and
those around me that I have always longed to do. Fear no longer holds me
because the love of God is now ruling in its place.

~ *Katelyn*

. . . .

Growing up, I was molested by the pastor of my church for 11 years. When I
finally told someone, they said it was my fault. On that same day, I gave away
my virginity and since then, tried to make sure I would never be hurt again.
Eventually, I chose to give my life to God, but it was hard to give my past to
Him because of this experience. I felt I was getting back at God for allowing
this to happen to me. When I began ministry school at the Ramp, we started
taking a class for women called Reinvent by Mrs. Lauren Bentley. At first, I
thought I didn't need it, but it didn't take long to realize this was exactly what
I needed. I needed healing. Taking Reinvent was an amazing, life changing
experience. She told me that my worth is so much more precious than what
I thought about myself. What would it look like to live a pure life? Does
purity mean virginity? What if I lost my virginity, can I get it back? These
questions kept going on in my head, and it was overwhelming me. This class
answered my questions and gave me a new perspective about myself. I know
how much God loves me! I am fearfully and wonderfully made in His image.
I am beautiful, and I live a life of purity!

~ *Andrea*

For as long as I can remember, I was bound in fear and thought of myself as insignificant before God. I didn't believe that I had a voice to Him or anyone else. During my first year, at the same time I was taking Reinvent, someone gave me a word from The Lord saying, "God loves to hear you sing." I'm not a singer at all, but I do love to sing during worship. They had no idea that I had been feeling so insignificant in this area. This word so changed my life and my view of Father God and my significance to Him. Immediately after this happened, I took the Reinvent class. Reinvent taught me more about breaking fear, knowing my identity and value, and good stewardship over these gifts of femininity and Godly womanhood.

The biggest thing that the Lord taught me through Reinvent was that my voice can change things. "Did you know your voice can shift atmospheres? Did you know that your confident prayers have the attention of God?" I remind myself of these things daily, and many more. I can confidently say that the Lord has set me free from fear in every way, and I now walk in wholeness. I am so thankful that I had the opportunity to take this class, and thank you Mrs. Lauren!

~ *Kayla*

Goodbye Girl
Hello Lady

GOODBYE, GIRL—HELLO, LADY

2020 © Copyright by Lauren Wheaton Bentley
Published by Ramp Media
122 Buckhorn Trail
Hamilton, AL 35570

Unless otherwise indicated, all Scripture quotations are taken from the Holy Bible, New Living Translation, copyright © 1996, 2004, 2015 by Tyndale House Foundation. Used by permission of Tyndale House Publishers, Inc., Carol Stream, Illinois 60188. All rights reserved.

Scripture quotations marked MSG are taken from THE MESSAGE, copyright © 1993, 1994, 1995, 1996, 2000, 2001, 2002 by Eugene H. Peterson. Used by permission of NavPress. All rights reserved. Represented by Tyndale House Publishers, Inc.

Scripture quotations marked NKJV are taken from the New King James Version®. Copyright © 1982 by Thomas Nelson. Used by permission. All rights reserved.

Scripture quotations marked TPT are from The Passion Translation®. Copyright © 2017, 2018 by Passion & Fire Ministries, Inc. Used by permission. All rights reserved. ThePassionTranslation.com.

Edited by Edie Mourey (www.furrowpress.com)
Cover Design and Interior Design by Brianna Showalter

Cover photography by Beau Hatton, Cypress + Light

ISBN: 978-1-7321827-3-8

Acknowledgements

Samuel—Your love has been a healing balm to my heart. You have allowed me to process through deep hurts and have shared mountain-top victories with me. I am now able to share those victories with others because you fought alongside me. Your ear to hear the voice of the Lord and your heart to obey Him sets the foundation for our family. I'm so thankful you gave me a second thought in the hallway of Hamilton High School. I love you forever.

Mom and Mama Nell—This book is simply a collection of the wisdom you have taught me. None of this could have been written without your example and guidance. Thank you for being patient with me in every season and for living with a pure heart before the Lord. You are the two most beautiful women in the world. I love you so much.

Lydia and Caroline—This book is a gift to you from my heart. It is full of truths I pray you believe about yourself both as my daughters and as daughters of God. You delight my heart and radiate God's beauty all around you. I pray these words become a part of who you are as women of God. You are so dearly loved.

William and Jonathan—Determined defender and God's gift. That's what your names mean, and that's who you are. You probably won't be too interested in reading this book, but your future wives better be! Thank you for praying over me and being honorable not just to me, but to all the women in your life. I love you so much.

Rick—I am so thankful God put you in my life. He knew how much I needed you. Thank you for believing in me, leading me, and loving me well. Your wisdom and support are gifts in my life. I love you so much.

Lindsey—My dear little Peacot, Elsa, AND Anna. We share the memories of many of the stories in this book in a way that no one else could. That's what sisters are for, right? God knew we would need someone to experience the exact same first 18 or so years of life not only for survival, but also for the ability to laugh through some of the harder parts. Thanks for forgiving me for being so mean to you when we were young. I'm glad we turned out friends. Love you lots.

The Bentleys and McCoys—Thank you for picking me out for Samuel and helping him win my heart. Each of you are gifts from Heaven to me. I am so thankful we are family. I love being a Bentley!

All my best girl friends—It's the best feeling in the world to know you have friends believing in you and pushing you past your comfort zone. From emotional breakdowns in your living rooms to Marco Polos across the world to laughing too loud in the office to napping during marathons, I am thankful for each one of you. You are life, hope, joy, and strength to me.

Edie—This book would be nothing close to what it is without your voice. You know just the right questions to ask to point me in the right direction and spur creativity. I could not have anticipated how working with you as an editor would bless me with such a wonderful gift of friendship. I'm also thankful to have vicariously enjoyed a lovely New York white Christmas. You and your family are dear to my heart.

Dan DePriest—Thank you for taking the reins and making this dream something I can hold in my hands. You've been a dream to work with. I am so thankful for you and Scribe Books.

To all my Reinvent students—When this class begins each semester, the syllabus states the course requirement is a willingness to be honest with yourself and delve into sometimes deeply personal issues. You always amaze me with the openness you bring to the classroom and a sincere desire to be taught what it looks like to be a Woman of God. This book is a gift to each of you. Thank you for allowing me to teach you. Remember, you CAN live a life free from fear.

CONTENTS

Foreword

I remember the first time I met the author of this book. Actually, it was quite a shock! The year was 1983, and I was pregnant with my first child. The ultrasound had clearly shown the baby inside me was a boy. As I stared at the blurry images on the black and white screen, I began secretly fighting a bit of disappointment since I had always dreamed of having a girl. In fact, I had ask God very specifically for a blonde-headed, blue-eyed girl with dimples. I left the doctors office and decided to "get in the boy spirit" by going shopping to buy boy clothes. Thankfully, I found a baby store that was going out of business! I purchased enough (non-returnable) boy clothes to fill the closet!

The next few months, I surrounded my life with blue. Finally, on April 13th, I gave my last push and heard the sweet cry of a baby and the words, "It's a GIRL!" As they laid her trembling body on top of mine, I looked down at her to see her blonde hair, blue eyes, and one dimple. I remember my first thought, "Delight yourself in the Lord, and He will give you the desires of your heart." I named her Lauren.

Since that day, I was privileged to have a front-row seat in this theater called "Life" as Lauren has lived out each scene described on the pages of this book. It has been a fascinating drama indeed! Lost in the wonder of the story, I cheered her on as she discovered her inner strength, wept when she felt the pain of insecurity, laughed when she danced with unbridled confidence, prayed as she fought her enemies, and sat amazed as she was transformed from an unsure, timid girl to an unwavering, victorious lady.

When God looks at you, He likes what He sees. He made you just the way He wanted you to be. Nothing God has ever done or created was "by accident." Every part of your life is filled with purpose. In other words, you matter. You are filled with gifts, ideas, beauty, and abilities that no one else has. You are uniquely designed by God, and it brings Him great pleasure to see you walk in the fullness of His dream for you.

But there is something you must remember. Just like Lauren and each one of us since Eve, you too have an enemy. His greatest intent is to keep you from knowing the love of your Father, and his second is to keep you from fulfilling the purpose for which you were created. In fact, satan's greatest fear is that you would believe what God has said about you.

From the wisdom of her personal devotion and her experience on the battlefield, Lauren is going to teach you how to recognize this thief hiding in the shadows. She will help train your ear to recognize his deceiving voice and put proven weapons in your hand to assure your victory. Through the promises and principles in this book, you will be awakened to a confidence and strength that comes from within. You will no longer find it necessary to strive for acceptance from the world around you, for you too are being transformed from the fearful girl you were to the valiant lady you are becoming.

Come now, I would like to invite you to join me in this grand theater. In fact, there's a seat right here beside me. With the turn of the page, the curtain will rise, and you will experience the transformation into everything God has intended you to be.

Karen Wheaton

Introduction

Reinvent

"What would your life look like without fear?"

That's the question a close friend asked me. I was twenty-eight years of age at the time and had no concept of who I was without fear, let alone what my life might look like without its companionship.

Whatever talents I had been given, opportunities I had considered, or thoughts of what I could do had all first passed under fear's scrutiny. Fear would evaluate who I could talk to. It would fact-check what others told me was true. It would dictate who was reliable and trustworthy. It would tell me how to behave. It even led me to believe it had my best interest in mind—that it was trying to preserve my reputation and keep me from looking different or crazy to everyone else.

My Introduction

I remember the first day fear became a part of my life. In fact, I know the exact date: October 14, 1987. I was four and a half years old, sitting on the floor as my grandparents watched the news. Baby

Jessica McClure had fallen into a well in her aunt's backyard in Midland, Texas. For more than two days, the paramedics worked feverishly to free her. The news media covered the story so well I felt as if I had been in the backyard with them, hearing her whimpers and seeing the rescue team with their eyes riveted on that narrow hole in the ground. I imagined how scary it must have been to be stuck, seeing only mud around you and no way out. I wondered if there were any wells in my own backyard.

Although her story had a wonderful ending, with Jessica being rescued from that muddy well, I had become absolutely terrified from watching the situation unfold. From that day on, I was scared to walk alone down the hallway to the bathroom or go to sleep by myself.

Sadly, it was not a phase I outgrew a few months later. No, I had been introduced to fear, and it barged right through the door of my heart, bringing its co-conspirators—insecurity and insignificance—along with it. On that fall day in 1987, fear became a cruel dictator in my life. It was twenty-four years later that my friend asked me, "Lauren, what would your life look like without fear?" It was not only my friend asking; it was the Holy Spirit. You know those moments—when it's not a matter of coming up with a great-sounding answer. The Holy Spirit is hoping you will stop long enough to really ponder the question He's asking.

As I considered my answer over the next couple of weeks, I realized something. I had believed fear was invincible. I had never considered there could be a day fear would no longer dominate my life. Everything was about to change, however. No matter what it looked like, I had to be free of this thing, this enemy . . . forever.

The Reinvented Life

Several years ago, I began teaching a class of college-aged women at the Ramp School of Ministry (RSM) in Hamilton, Alabama. I titled the class, "Reinvent." I love what the definition of that word means for us women who have struggled with confidence. To reinvent means to make, as if for the first time, something already created or invented. God did not create us to live with a spirit of fear. In 2 Timothy 1:7, it is made very clear that fear and timidity do not come from Him: "For God has not given us a spirit of fear and timidity, but of power, love, and self-discipline." Fear, insecurity, and insignificance all come when we begin to listen to the false voices around us—or even within us (we'll talk more about that later).

In the pages that follow, you will learn how to overcome the things keeping you from being a woman of purpose, discover who you are meant to be, and begin to live confidently and victoriously as was intended by the Father.

This book is written in two parts, the first titled "Goodbye, Girl" and the second "Hello, Lady." In Part 1, you will say goodbye to fear, insecurity, and insignificance. In Part 2, you will say hello to God's idea of beauty, purity, and confidence. At the end of each chapter, I've included a section titled "Know the Voice," which I pray will encourage you to approach each of these topics in your own heart and life. This will provide you with an opportunity to:

- reflect on whose voice you're hearing and how that has impacted you,
- remember what the Holy Spirit wants you to know,
- and respond to His Voice through prayer or declaration.

Before we go any further, I want to ask you this question: Are you ready to say goodbye to the girl you've been and hello to the confident lady Father God has destined you to become? If you are, then let's go! But if you're still not sure, I encourage you to read on with me anyway. You just may become empowered to overcome fear, begin to live boldly, and walk in victory.

Part One:
Goodbye, Girl

Letting Go of Fear, Insecurity, and Insignificance

"Beloved ones, with promises like these, and because of our deepest respect and worship of God, we must remove everything from our lives that contaminates body and spirit, and continue to complete the development of holiness within us."

—1 Cor 7:1 TPT

CHAPTER ONE

Unfriend Fear

We all have that first vague memory, the memory that belongs to us because it is our own and not prompted from a photograph we've looked at through the years. I shared my first memory with you. But I was wondering if you remember when you were introduced to fear. When did you first meet our mutual "friend"?

Perhaps your introduction came later in life. Maybe you didn't become acquainted until early adolescent or teen years. You see, fear capitalizes on what should be a passing moment, as though it recognizes the opportunity to knock at your door. It's a thought, then a question, that becomes a road paved of worst-case scenarios and "what-ifs." It will show up at your door anytime it wants, no matter who you are, where you are, or what you're doing. It pushes its way in without even a knock, "Is anyone home?" or "How do you do?"

When fear entered my life, I was relieved to have something that didn't mind if I hid behind it. I thought it wanted to keep me safe and secure. It would know what was good for me, keep me from being hurt, and blend me into the crowd so I wouldn't stick out. Fear was there for me where no one else could be.

There was only one problem, however. There was one Person in my life who didn't like my friend, and that Person was God. In fact, fear is one of God's enemies. Fear is a spirit. And the spirit of fear is not and was not there to protect me. It was sent to destroy me and God's destiny for my life. I believe it was sent to you to do the same.

Identity Theft

There are two lies the spirit of fear works hard to make you believe. The first is that you're alone—that no one experiences the intensity of fear you live with every day. The second is that fear cannot be overcome. It is invincible and will always be a part of your life. It needs you to believe these lies because it does not want you to see how weak and fragile it actually is.

Fear asserts itself in every thought we have, decision we make, or activity we do. It even hacks into and reprograms our belief system. It says in the most convincing way, "You're too quiet to do anything truly great. Everybody sees you as completely ordinary. You don't have any talents. You can't do anything right. You're always in the way and messing things up. You're a failure. That's what you are—a failure."

Fear's voice is loud and its accusation persuasive. In the moment, what it's saying seems like the truest thing in the world. It creates such a noisy chaos in our minds, like a form of sonic terrorism, resulting in a decision-making paralysis of sorts. What we should do or would enjoy doing seems impossible as the voice inside overwhelms us. We are not ourselves anymore. Our identity has been hijacked.

Dodge Ball Dreams

Physical Education (PE) in school was absolute torture for me. Every activity was a challenge, but one particular game would plunge me into despair: dodge ball. Life didn't get any worse than dodge ball day for Lauren, age ten. The first few times, I told my teacher I had a terrible stomach ache. This worked beautifully until he caught on to my desperate attempts to escape playing. I had to come up with another solution.

The next few times we played, I tried to walk calmly out of the game, regardless of whether or not I had been hit by a ball. It was a miracle! No one seemed to notice, and my teammates certainly didn't miss my contribution. Then, one day, my worst nightmare became a reality. I didn't make it to the sideline in time. There were too few people on my team for me just to walk out of the game without being hit, and if I tried, my teacher might say something in front of everyone. I was standing as far away from the middle line as possible, trying to jump in front of the flying balls. They were all too fast for me. Suddenly, there were two people left in the game: me and the kid on the other team. My teammates were screaming at me to throw a ball. I could win the game if I just threw a ball and hit the kid. The problem was I couldn't move.

You've been there before, haven't you? When everything goes into slow motion and all eyes are watching to see what you will do with this moment? Will you come through and save the day, or will you shrink back and do nothing?

The gym lights dim, and the spotlight flips on as you wrestle with two distinct sounds in your head: the screaming taunts of fear and the pounding of your heartbeat. As the imaginary camera pans across the kids' faces on the sideline, there's that glimpse of a different version of yourself—determination squints your eyes as you shake off the intimidation and take one heavy step after another toward the ball. With the form of an olympian, you hurl it across the gym, watching it arch through the air. A shocked opponent falls to his knees in defeat. The whole school goes wild! They sling you up on their shoulders, chanting your name, and the rest of the year, everyone begs you to play on their team. You are the Dodgeball Queen, and nothing will ever scare you again.

You can probably imagine none of this is what happened to me in PE that day. At least my torment did not last forever—although in the moment, I would have argued that point. I was an easy target, standing motionless and breathless in front of my opponent. The ball finally hit me—for real this time—and the game was over.

Now, friend, I have not needed dodgeball skills one time in my adulthood. Not. Once. Could there not have been an option to play with that round, rainbow-colored parachute for those of us who lacked in athleticism? That was still physical activity and not emotionally traumatizing, but that's beside the point.

Taking Back Your Life

We miss out on so many opportunities to do something for others, for God, or simply for the fun of it because we're consumed by the shouts of fear in our own minds, but things *can* change. You *can* take back what the voice has stolen. You *can* shut down fear's noisy charade. You *can* say goodbye to the girl who has cowered down and lived under fear's tyranny. And the lady you occasionally watch in slow motion—the one who knows what to do and overcomes every obstacle in her way—that, my friend, is who you really are.

Allow me to officially introduce you. This lady is the one who embodies God's design for her. She's found her significance in Him. She's comfortable in her own skin. She's redefined beauty and embraced purity. She's confident and strong. She has appeared for brief moments in your heart before jumping back behind all the things you'd have to confront to reach her. Now that you see her, do you really want to continue to shrink back and hide in the shadows of fear, insecurity, or insignificance? After all, these enemies are not invincible. In fact, they have already been defeated! It is time to say goodbye to the girl fear has painted as yourself and get to know this lady who has been calling to you. Remember, God your Father, "has not given you a spirit of fear, but of power, love, and a sound mind" (2 Tim 1:7). The timid version of yourself is a false identity. This confident version of yourself is the *real you.*

Our True Friend and Helper

As we confront fear and its co-conspirators, there is one companion we must have. We need the Holy Spirit; in fact, we can't overcome these false friends without His help. When Jesus was preparing His disciples for His death, resurrection, and ascension, He told them it was better for Him to leave so that the Holy Spirit could come.

Better? Did He say it would be better for Him to leave? How could it be better? the disciples must have thought. After all, they had only spent a few years with Jesus. They were still learning His ways and, quite frankly, were easily thrown off by things He did or said. The disciples were yet experiencing moments when they didn't understand His teaching. And He was going to leave because it would be better for them?

Yes, it would be better for them because Jesus' departure meant the Holy Spirit, another Helper like Him, could then come. The Holy Spirit would be the promised Friend and Comforter who would live within them. One of the Holy Spirit's roles would be to lead and guide the disciples into all truth (John 16:13). The law that was once written on tablets of stone would now be written upon the disciples' hearts (2 Cor 3:3). The Holy Spirit would be faithful to remind them of all Jesus said and with it would provide understanding of Jesus' words (John 14:26).

Now, the Holy Spirit is in you to enable you to become and do all that the Father has destined for you. The Great Designer of the Universe fashioned you in His image, showed you His great love through the sacrifice of His Son, and equipped you with everything you need and the power to become the lady He intended you to be through His Holy Spirit.

No matter what situation you are in, if the Holy Spirit is nudging you to step out in faith, He will back up your act of obedience with His supernatural power. You will never regret obeying His voice—even if the outcome doesn't look exactly like you thought it would. Even if it seems nothing else is accomplished, the act of obeying the voice of the Holy Spirit in itself will bring victory in your life over the voices of fear, insecurity, and insignificance. If, on the other hand, you allow these voices to take this opportunity from you, the noise of the moment will eventually settle back down, and you'll be left wondering what could have happened if you simply had obeyed.

As we begin this journey together, we need the Holy Spirit to remind us of who we really are. We need Him to make sure there is no place left hidden, still occupied by a spirit of fear. The Holy Spirit will strengthen you with a strong sense of purpose and the confidence to do what you were called to do. You can live empowered to be all God has ordained you to be, doing all that He has called you to do.

So, are you ready to unfriend fear, expose insecurity, and silence insignificance? Are you ready to say goodbye, once and for all, to that voice of fear and to the false identity it created? Do you want to take this journey to discover the lady who lives inside you, bold and courageous, free from fear, and full of God? I am so excited to meet the real you. Let's do this!

Know the Voice

REFLECT

- What is the first experience you can remember having with fear? How has it impacted your life?
- Write down three words:

  A word that best describes you: _____

  A word that others might use to describe you:

  _____

  A word that describes the person you want to be:

  _____

REMEMBER

- Fear is an enemy of God's. It is a spirit, and it is not your friend.
- On index cards or sticky notes, write down the word you used above to describe the person you want to be and place it on the mirror of your bathroom, the glove compartment

of your car, and/or the door of your refrigerator. Let this be a reminder that, through the power of the Holy Spirit, you *can* be the person you feel called to be.

- "For God will never give you the spirit of fear, but the Holy Spirit who gives you mighty power, love, and self-control" (2 Tim 1:7 TPT).

RESPOND

Father God,

I recognize that fear is not a gift from You, but instead, it is an enemy sent to destroy Your destiny for my life. I repent for believing the lies fear has spoken to me and ask that the Holy Spirit would restore my mind to think according to Your will. Establish my identity in who You have called me to be and give me strength to recognize every time fear tries to reenter my thoughts. I ask all these things in the name of Jesus who has conquered fear forever. Amen.

CHAPTER TWO

Confront the Bully

My first name is Lauren. It comes from the Latin word *laurel*, which is the leaf that made up the crowns worn by ancient Greek victors and is recognized worldwide as a symbol of victory. In simple terms, my name means *victorious woman*.

There have been times when the meaning has seemed far removed from who I have been. More recently, though, the meaning of my name has come to play a significant role in my life because it has given me hope. It has stirred my faith that I will not only walk in victory over the enemies that have held me back, but I also will see many other women overcome those enemies. After all, Jesus has made *us* more than conquerers (Rom 8:37). So, *we*—you and I—are victorious women!

A few years ago, if you had told me there would come a day I would write a book about overcoming fear, I would not have had the self-confidence to speak with you let alone the faith to believe you. I was too shy. In fact, I was so shy that a childhood friend recently reconnected with me and said, "I used to think I'd have to put change in you to make you talk. You were so quiet!"

Deep down inside, however, especially throughout my school years, I wanted to be popular. I wanted to be one of those girls who knew the right things to say, wore the right clothes, and commanded the hallway as I walked self-confidently passed my fellow students at the end of the school day. Sadly, it was never to be. I would hardly speak up at all, much less take risks and set some kind of social standard. Fear was safe. After all, no one expects much out of the shy girl.

My sister, Lindsey, was three years younger than me. Although her personality was much more outgoing and less fearful, thankfully, she wasn't popular either, so at least I had someone I could try out some of my "cool" quips and phrases on. I would give her "cool lessons" and call her "girlfriend" in the sassiest tone I could muster, but only in the safety of my own bedroom. Somehow, I tricked her into believing I was popular and uber-cool enough to teach her my hip ways. (Please, don't let her read this. I think she may still believe me.)

When I was in third grade, Lindsey and I started a new school. Up until that point, we had attended a small, private, Christian school. There were many students in my new class! Butterflies filled my stomach every day as I walked into Mrs. Busing's classroom. She was a wonderful teacher, gentle and understanding, who instilled in me a lifelong love for reading. She (and my crush, Scott) made school tolerable enough.

At the end of the year, she worked with the other teachers to put together a program that featured the third grade students. I was given a solo. I was to sing "The Lonely Goatherd." Yes, it was the yodeling song Julie Andrews and her onscreen Von Trapp family sang during the puppet show in the movie, *The Sound of Music*. Now, I am not nor have I ever been a yodeler, "Lay dee odl lay ee-hoo." I don't know why I was chosen for this part or why the shy girl was given the yodeling solo, but there was one very happy woman in the audience—Karen Wheaton, my mother!

I remember standing in my authentic-looking Austrian dress, sewn from scratch, with my hair curled and back-combed to highest perfection. The year was 1992, and big hair still reigned supreme in Alabama. My song came on, and there I stood center stage in front of the entire third grade and all the parents, grandparents, aunts, uncles, and school staff. A bit petrified, I was able to sing out the first verse and chorus. But somewhere mid-yodel, it happened. My voice cracked. Out came a dreadful noise that sounded more like the goat than the goatherd!

I can't tell you what happened next because it was forever lost to me. All I could think of was how awful I must have sounded to everyone. The only thing etched in my memory is what occurred as I walked offstage.

One of the boys from my class told me I ruined the entire play. His words pierced my eight-year-old heart and replayed in my mind for the next twenty years. In fact, it was one of the first things I thought about those twenty years later when my friend asked me what my life would look like without fear.

A Mouse with a Microphone

I never quite answered my friend, but her question set my life on an unanticipated trajectory. Not long after, I attended a Jesus Culture event in Chicago, Illinois. Reinhard Bonnke, the great evangelist, spoke during the conference. I will never forget his words: "Some Christians live in a room—a very dark room—and they hear a lion, roaring in the darkness. They say, 'Oh, I am so afraid! I will be eaten by this lion!' Then someone turns on the light switch, and they see it is just a mouse with a microphone. That is the voice of fear in your life."

In that moment, I knew God was doing something supernatural in me. The light switch had been flipped. The spirit of fear was exposed as nothing more than a bully—a voice with no real power. It had all been a façade. This voice that had kept me held back, had kept me from doing what I felt called by God to do, had kept me hidden and quiet—the voice that did not want me to become the woman I so wanted to be—*that* voice was a mouse with a microphone! And to beat it all, I had been sacrificing my purpose to its lies.

Suddenly, I could see how time after time I had relinquished myself to its control. Every time the Holy Spirit had drawn me to pray with someone I didn't know or had nudged me to take a risk in simply being myself in front of other people or even in a situation as fun and simple as playing dodgeball with my classmates, the spirit of fear—that ridiculous mouse—had convinced me to cower back. It had taken over my thoughts and shut me down. Moment by moment, my life was being stolen from me.

As I began to realize what the spirit of fear had taken from me, a determination came over me. It was more than determination. I was outright furious. I felt used and manipulated. Fear had lied to me, and I had believed it. When I realized that, there was nothing I wouldn't do to walk in victory over this enemy, because that is exactly what it had become—an enemy. I love when David says to God in Psalm 139:22, "Your enemies are my enemies, and I hate them with a perfect hatred." Realizing once again that fear is an enemy of God's, I got on God's side against His enemy who had become my enemy, too!

When I came home from the conference, there was something I knew I had to do: I had to sing, even if I only sang one song just once. I contacted the worship leader at the Ramp who, at the time, was Bryn Waddell, and he agreed to meet with me.

Getting Back the Microphone

I remember sitting down with Bryn in his office to describe what God was doing in my heart and explain why singing seemed to be part of this journey for me. He was very gracious and understanding. He even let me learn a song with the band that—if the moment was right—I would possibly sing during the worship set of an upcoming conference.

A few weeks later, the Ramp held its annual women's conference. It's hosted by my mother. Several hundred women attended the conference, and I was there, ready to experience victory over this enemy. My enemy. God's enemy. In the middle of one of the worship sets, Bryn and my mom invited me to the stage to share what I had experienced. Trembling from head to toe, I told the story of the boy in third grade and how those words had echoed in my mind for twenty years. I shared how the curtain had been pulled on the spirit of fear in my life and how this mouse with a microphone had taken control of my life. And then, I sang. I mean, I *sang*! The Presence of the Holy Spirit was tangible in that moment. He came, and not only was I, but many other women there were set free from fear that day!

When I walked off the stage, my husband, Samuel, was waiting for me. He had been encouraging me all along and knew the huge victory that had just been won. Bryn walked up, and as he hugged me, he said, "I believe in you." I knew it was the voice of the Father bringing that third-grade moment full circle. The Father replaced the lies I had believed since a child of not being good enough or talented with this simple truth: He, the Creator of the Universe, believes in me.

Looking back, I'm amazed at God's justice and, dare I say, vengeance against His enemy. Twenty years after the enemy took my microphone out of my hand and began using it to torment me with his voice, God took the microphone from my enemy's hand and put it right back into my hand! Now, whenever I get up to teach, lead, or even just hang out with my friends, I can easily recognize when fear tries to shut me down. Today, once I recognize the voice, I remember the victory God won for me and choose which voice I will obey. What God did for me, He will do for you as you dare to obey His Voice.

It's Time to Confront Fear

I have to say it again: Fear is an enemy of God's. Therefore, it is your enemy. Although it's easy to think fear is just part of your personality, it's not. Remember, fear is a spirit, and it is holding you back from all the things you know you are meant to accomplish. Your Heavenly Father sent you with purpose, talents, abilities, and destiny. The enemy wants to be sure you never realize them! Your victory is assured when you are willing to confront the areas you've allowed fear to rule in your life. If you don't know where to begin, or how to take back the microphone, allow me to make a suggestion. Really ask yourself this question: What would your life look like if fear had no place in you?

Did you see her? Even if just for a moment? Did you catch that little glimpse of her? That version of you, bold, victorious, and confident—head held high, assured of yourself, your worth, your significance?

That lady, my friend, is you. The *real* you.

Maybe it's the first time you've ever seen your true self. That's okay. It's actually the best place to begin. You see, now you know the thing keeping you from becoming that victorious woman is your enemy—the spirit of fear, that little mouse with a microphone. Keep this new image in front of yourself to remember there *is* something worth fighting for. *She* is worth fighting for.

Know the Voice

REFLECT

- What would your life look like if fear had no place in you?
- What would confronting the bully of fear look like in your life? What would you have to do?
- What will you do with that microphone now in your hand?

REMEMBER

- Fear wants you to believe that you cannot overcome it—that it's impossible. But Jesus has already won that victory for you.
- The real you—the you free from fear—is worth fighting for.
- "Then Jesus made a public spectacle of all the powers and principalities of darkness, stripping away from them every weapon and all their spiritual authority and power to accuse us. And by the power of the cross, Jesus led them around

as prisoners in a procession of triumph. He was not their prisoner; they were His!" (Col 2:15 TPT).

RESPOND

Father God,

Thank You for fighting the battle with fear and overcoming this enemy so I can walk in victory. Help me to uncover every root of fear and let nothing hidden remain. I don't want to hold anything back from You. There is nothing in my heart that is off limits to You. I choose to believe what You have spoken over my life and to let go of every fear that would keep me from becoming that person You've designed me to be, in the name of Jesus who has conquered fear forever. Amen!

CHAPTER THREE

Expose Insignificance

Sometimes, our enemies are obvious. I knew I was afraid before. The voice of fear was loud and familiar. After the Lord did so much in my heart to set me free from the control of that fear, I then knew how to recognize when it was speaking.

Other enemies are not as obvious, however. Insignificance was that enemy for me. I didn't know I had been listening to its voice until it was exposed in an unexpectedly beautiful moment of victory. In that moment, I discovered there are some battles God fights for us without us even knowing there is a war going on. Our only responsibility is to celebrate His victory! With a God like that, what else is there to do but worship, praise, and live all our lives for Him? At least that's all I could do after I found He had fought and won a battle for me.

An Exciting Invitation

I was in my office working through dozens of emails. An email from Tiffany Cochran came in, and I opened it immediately. At the time, Tiffany was Havilah Cunnington's assistant. Havilah is one of my favorite ministers. She is based out of Bethel Church in Redding, California, and travels the world as what she calls a *Word Girl*. She is a powerful and dynamic teacher. The email was an invitation to my mom, Catherine Mullins (the Ramp's worship leader at that time), and me to attend Bethel's women's conference titled *Wonder*.

My mom was ministering in England and couldn't attend, so Catherine and I flew to California to worship with our extended Christian family at Bethel Church. At one point during the first night, Havilah asked us to think about what we hoped to receive from the Lord during the weekend. I really thought about that for a bit. What did I want from this weekend? What was my heart really searching for? It didn't take long for me to have my answer. "God, I want to have a better understanding of who You are as my Father."

Maybe that sounds childish and spiritually immature, especially for someone who has been in or around the ministry her entire life. But for years, there had been something missing in my relationship with God. Though I knew Him as Savior and Lord, I grappled with this question: What does it mean to be loved by God as Father? It was something I just couldn't wrap my mind around.

Many people, including Christians, have what some call a *father-shaped hole* in their hearts. Perhaps their earthly fathers were not present in their lives, or maybe they were simply imperfect in relating to them. The result is the same: a hurting son or daughter—a child who longs to be accepted and loved wholly, to know his or her worth.

I had that hole in my heart. My parents divorced when I was twelve years old. The relationship with my father has seen ups and downs ever since then, but things really went downhill in my adulthood. At the time of the trip to California, my father and I had not spoken in two years. I knew if I could go home from the weekend with a better understanding of God and His Father's-heart toward me, it would mean a huge life victory for me. I would pray differently if I understood the way God felt about me. I might even be able to relate to those worship songs about what a wonderful Father He is.

The next day, Catherine and I went into the conference ready to be sponges and soak up all the wisdom, the glorious worship, and everything else the Holy Spirit had for us. During one of the sessions, a woman named Abi Stumvall shared her story. As an illustration, she had a man stand on one side of the stage to represent the way we imagine God thinks toward us. His arms were crossed, his face scowled, and he just looked angry, frustrated, and disappointed. I knew immediately this was the way I imagined Father God.

On the other side of the stage, Abi's husband represented God, and two other people represented Jesus and the Holy Spirit. They stood together and displayed an environment filled with love, where not only they were fully loved and celebrated themselves, but also they were inviting us into that fellowship with them to be fully loved and celebrated. At one point, Abi pulled the man representing Jesus to the other side of the stage. Hiding behind him, she talked about how she had believed a lie that the only way God could love and approve of her was if He could look at Jesus and not have to see her at all. With Jesus as a shield to protect her from the wrath God must feel toward her imperfections and failures, maybe, just maybe, God could accept her.

It was the inner workings of my own outlook toward God laid bare in front of me. I knew God was answering the question I had asked the night before: What does it mean to be loved by Him as Father?

At the end of the message, Abi's husband asked anyone who had wounds from their natural father to stand so he could pray over them. I was a bit embarrassed to stand because I am a minister. I thought I should have been beyond father issues at that stage of my life. I also knew it was a God moment, and I did not want to miss a single thing He had for me on that trip! I stood, and Abi's husband began to not only pray, but to apologize as a representative of an earthly father for so many different areas of pain in people's lives. He said, "I am sorry I wasn't there when you needed me to be. I am sorry I was so focused on my career I couldn't see you. I am sorry I was not able to control my anger."

It was a very deep and tender moment with the Holy Spirit. I'm not one to be hugely emotional or responsive in moments like that, but tears came and quietly melted away the hurt I had felt. I knew God was healing places in me I could never reach on my own. He was pouring in liquid love, the ointment I needed, into the father-shaped hole in my heart. I felt opened and vulnerable in a good way—free to receive His love and even share it with others.

If you have experienced wounds from your earthly father, I encourage you to ask God to reveal Himself as Father to you. It will take an open heart and faith to believe He will speak to you. But I believe—*I know*—if you will "come close to God, God will come close to you" (Jas 4:8). I know this is easier said than done because it took so long for me to be willing to admit there was an emptiness in my heart and to admit I had not allowed God to fill it. It's not like that was the first message I had heard on the love of God as Father; it was just the first time I had allowed my heart to be opened and changed by hearing the truth of His love toward me.

When you are ready to receive healing, all you have to do is open your heart. God is ready to reveal Himself to you. So many times, He's waiting on us to let the walls down. After that experience, I now know He can come to us when we aren't even expecting Him to, and He can prepare us to receive the healing we need.

When the session was over, I felt very close to Father God. I felt as though I were a part of that family Abi had demonstrated on stage with God, Jesus, and the Holy Spirit. I was welcomed. I was loved. I was accepted. I was wanted. And I was not a disappointment.

A Surprise Victory

The next day of conference, I was on my own. Catherine had a ministry date scheduled before we received the invitation to California, so she had to fly out early that morning. I went to the auditorium ready for another day of receiving everything God had for me. The morning sessions were being taught by some of my favorite women in ministry. I took pages of notes on redefining success, on believing more in who God called me to be, and on raising children who are passionate for Jesus.

At lunch, I went to the green room where we had been invited to eat with the Bethel staff and team. I was having a wonderful conversation with a pastor's wife from North Carolina and some leaders in Bethel's School of Supernatural Ministry when Havilah walked out of a side, private room, where she was eating with some of the leadership from Bethel. She walked up to my table and said, "Lauren, when you finish eating, come in here with us. I'd like you to meet some more of our team."

I sat for a few more minutes, moving the food around on my plate and preparing myself to be as normal as possible. I was about to enter a room in which there were these people I so look up to—individuals who have influenced and challenged me to become more. I have to admit I was intimidated at the thought of meeting them! But soon, I excused myself and headed toward the door through which Havilah had returned.

I walked in the room and up to the table where Havilah was sitting. She motioned for me to sit down beside her, and I looked around the table and saw many wonderful ministers. The intimidation I had felt only moments before was gone. In its place was an almost overwhelming feeling of acceptance and love by not only the honor of the initial invitation to attend the conference, but also by the invite to sit at the lunch table with these leaders. God's message was clear. There was a seat for me at the table—not because I had impacted thousands of lives like they had or because I had acquired the level of ministry they had. There was a seat for me at that table because God wanted to shatter insignificance. He wanted to open my eyes to this enemy.

That night, I entered the service and went to my seat. Bethel Music was about to lead the worship set before Lisa Bevere shared the message. The atmosphere was filled with anticipation. It had been a glorious two days, and this was the cherry on top! There really is nothing like a room full of women worshipping Jesus together. There's a raw, real, passionate place that a woman can go to when she unites with other women to reach Jesus.

As different leaders walked to their seats around me, several took a moment to stop and speak with me and ask about the Ramp or my family. By the time worship started, I was undone as I thought, *God, is this what You think about me? You have a seat for me at that table? That*

I matter that much to You? Is this what You think about me? Because this is not what I have thought about myself.

In that moment of worship, the Holy Spirit revealed a grid of insignificance I had subconsciously built. I didn't see myself as a great minister, unusually talented, crazy anointed, or really anyone special at all. I was just me with more than my fair share of insecurities and plenty of room for improvement. If I were choosing my own place at a table, it would not have been with those people or in that room with those ministers who have accomplished so much for the Kingdom. But right then and there, God was revealing a stronghold of insignificance in my mind.

I know, I know what you may be thinking. Yes, I am my mother's daughter, and I have had her wonderful example and love. Shouldn't growing up as a minister's daughter silence all those questions of significance? Am I implying significance is measured by the size of a ministry platform or by sitting at a table with those who have impacting ministries? The answer to all these questions is undoubtedly, "No!" This was simply the circumstance the Holy Spirit used to expose the grid of insignificance in my heart and mind.

Significance is an *internal* issue—not the size of your audience, your popularity among your peers, the number of your Instagram followers, or the reach of your ministry. Significance is measured by obedience to the Holy Spirit. When you walk in submission to the Holy Spirit, He transforms what seems like an ordinary moment into something with *eternal* consequence and meaning. When you realize the weightiness of that responsibility, everything you do becomes significant. Every moment is an opportunity for you to walk in obedience to the Holy Spirit and to step into the eternal work He is doing on the earth.

The Holy Spirit is working *through you.* Who you are and what you do are not about a big name or platform ministry; they're not about the expectations others may put on you because of the way you were raised—either for good or bad. Who you are and what you do are about being God's child and walking in obedience to what He has called you to do in every moment.

The significance of your life becomes dependent on your consistent *yes* to Him. Because He is God, because He has made you, because He has called you according to His purposes, you are significant. And what you do in obedience to Him has value and worth in His eyes.

Know the Voice

REFLECT

- What is the image that comes to mind when you see Father God? Is He cold, distant, and harsh, or is He warm, loving, and kind?
- How has your relationship with your earthly father influenced the way you perceive God?

- How has insignificance impacted the way you view yourself? Do these thoughts line up with God's Word over your life?

REMEMBER

- God can win battles we don't even realize we're fighting. Hallelujah!
- Even the most amazing earthly fathers are imperfect. God wants to reveal His perfect love to you through faith.
- Significance is an internal issue. It is determined by your willingness to obey the Holy Spirit.

RESPOND

Father God,

Thank You for uncovering the enemy of insignificance that has kept me from believing what You have spoken over my life. Today, I choose to believe in the destiny You've purposed for me. I repent for any acts of disobedience to Your voice because of the belief in my own insignificance. Help me to believe in every dream You've planted within my heart and to recognize when and where the Holy Spirit is leading me. You are worthy of my trust, so I trust You with my life and purpose. Amen.

CHAPTER FOUR

Find Significance

When I came home from the trip to California, I began to delve into this idea of insignificance. It was new to me. Fear was an enemy I knew well because it had consumed my life for so long. As I mentioned before, I had no idea there was a stronghold of insignificance until it was exposed. I wanted to understand more so I could see what this enemy had been taking from me. After all, God is a God of restoration. If there were things that had been lost, I wanted them back!

I began studying different heroes of the Bible, and of course, one after another, I realized they were all "insignificant." From Moses with his speech impediment to Gideon, who was the least in his family, to David, the youngest of his brothers who tended his father's sheep—every hero I read about was someone who lacked the "it" factor. They would not have stood out in a crowd. They would have been easily overlooked. Perhaps they even preferred to remain hidden.

These were my kind of people. Each time God approached one of these men, He had to suffer through their excuses of insignificance before He could offer the remedy: "I am *with you*." God spoke those words to each one of them and so many more throughout Scripture.

Moses may have lacked in his ability to speak, but *with God*, he delivered Israel from the slavery of Egypt. Gideon did not have the family prestige to lead the army of Israel, but *with God*, the army of heaven was enlisted, and the Midianites were conquered. David lived in service to his father and older brothers, but *with God*, he defeated Goliath and was anointed king over Israel.

In all of this, I knew God was speaking to me. I still wondered, however, what insignificance had taken from me or—if it had been left hidden—what *could* it have taken from me? My question was answered in the story of Saul.

Baggage Claim

Saul's story begins in 1 Samuel 9 when the prophet Samuel was searching throughout Israel for a king. The Lord revealed to Samuel that Saul had been chosen. Samuel told Saul,

> "I am here to tell you that you and your family are the
> focus of all Israel's hopes." Saul replied, "But I'm only
> from the tribe of Benjamin, the smallest tribe in Israel,

and my family is the least important of all the families of that tribe! Why are you talking like this to me?" Then Samuel brought Saul and his servant into the hall and placed them at the head of the table, honoring them above the thirty special guests. (1 Sam 9:20–22)

In the next chapter, we are told that Samuel privately anointed Saul king with a flask of olive oil, and then he sent Saul back home. Afterwards, Samuel gathered all the tribes of Israel together to reveal their king:

> Later Samuel called all the people of Israel to meet before the Lord at Mizpah. And he said, "This is what the Lord, the God of Israel, has declared: I brought you from Egypt and rescued you from the Egyptians and from all of the nations that were oppressing you. But though I have rescued you from your misery and distress, you have rejected your God today and have said, 'No, we want a king instead!' Now therefore, present yourselves before the Lord by tribes and clans." So Samuel brought all the tribes of Israel before the Lord, and the tribe of Benjamin was chosen by lot. Then he brought each family of the tribe of Benjamin before the Lord, and the family of the Matrites was chosen. And finally Saul son of Kish was chosen from among them. But when they looked for him, he had disappeared! So they asked the Lord, "Where is he?" And

the Lord replied, "He is hiding among the baggage." So they found him and brought him out, and he stood head and shoulders above anyone else. Then Samuel said to all the people, "This is the man the Lord has chosen as your king. No one in all Israel is like him!" (1 Sam 10:17–24)

It's clear from this story that the voice of insignificance was overpowering Saul's mind. On his coronation day, the day he would be made the greatest leader in Israel—the first king!—he was found hiding among the baggage. Some things are just so obvious in the Bible that all you can do is smile.

Hidden away behind our baggage is exactly where insignificance wanted to keep you and me. Your baggage may be a strained relationship with your father like mine was, or it could be an addiction that has seemed impossible to break. It could be as hidden as a constantly negative attitude or as complex as a stronghold of fear. It could be past sins or present sins. Baggage is that voice in your mind that says, "You can't do anything for God. You haven't even dealt with your own issues yet."

That baggage can be based on truth. It's true that Moses had a speech impediment and was not the greatest communicator to stand before Pharaoh. Gideon's tribe truly was the weakest in Israel, and Saul's was the smallest. My relationship with my father is not what I wish it could be. There really was a stronghold of fear that kept me in bondage to its demands. However, these things did not disqualify the heroes of faith from being strong through God, and they will not stop you or me!

When God looks at us, He sees with different eyes. He's looking for someone through whom He may show Himself strong. Second Chronicles 16:9 tells us, "The eyes of the Lord search the whole earth in order to strengthen those whose hearts are fully committed to Him."

The woman whose heart is completely devoted to God finds her significance in Him. When God sees her heart is willing to obey Him and walk in relationship with Him, He shows Himself strong through her. God sees her heart's devotion as worthy of His attention, and she finds her sense of significance in His attention.

The Cost of Insignificance

Sadly, the story of Saul doesn't end with his being crowned king over Israel. Saul dealt with a mindset of insignificance throughout his reign.

In a story you may already be familiar with, Saul walked in outright disobedience to the command of the Lord. The Amalekites had opposed Israel when they came in from Egypt, and God wanted to settle the account. He specifically told Saul to destroy the entire Amalekite nation—men, women, children, and animals. Saul obeyed most of what the Lord had asked of him, but he spared Agag, the king of the Amalekites, as well as the best of the cattle. First Samuel 15:9 says Saul and his men spared everything that appealed to them. That night, the Lord revealed Saul's sin to the prophet Samuel. Early the next morning, Samuel set out to find King Saul.

When Samuel finally found him, Saul greeted him cheerfully. "May the Lord bless you," he said. "I have carried out the Lord's command!" "Then what is all the bleating of sheep and goats and the lowing of cattle I hear?" Samuel demanded. "It's true that the army spared the best of the sheep, goats, and cattle," Saul admitted. "But they are going to sacrifice them to the Lord your God. We have destroyed everything else." Then Samuel said to Saul, "Stop! Listen to what the Lord told me last night!" "What did he tell you?" Saul asked. And Samuel told him, "Although you may think little of yourself, are you not the leader of the tribes of Israel? The Lord has anointed you king of Israel. And the Lord sent you on a mission and told you, 'Go and completely destroy the sinners, the Amalekites, until they are all dead.' Why haven't you obeyed the Lord? Why did you rush for the plunder and do what was evil in the Lord's sight?" (1 Sam 15:13–19)

God knew the inner workings of Saul's heart and cut right to the chase in what He revealed to Samuel: "Although you may think little of yourself, are you not the leader of the tribes of Israel?

The Lord has anointed you king of Israel." *Insignificance* was at the heart of Saul's disobedience to the Lord's command. That one act of disobedience, rooted in the belief in his own insignificance, ultimately cost him the throne of Israel. At the end of this story, God rejected Saul as king.

The throne is not the only thing Saul lost at the hand of insignificance. God was looking for not only a king over Israel, but a friend—someone who would partner with Him—to shepherd His people with a pure heart. A man after His own heart. Someone God could build a lasting dynasty from. God had wanted Saul to be that person, but it was not to be. Saul could not overcome his internal insignificance—no matter how great his external position. He couldn't recognize the call was to lead the people *with God*. He wanted to lead the people in his own strength.

David was a different kind of king over Israel. He learned dependence on God when he killed the lion and the bear that tried to take his father's sheep. He knew a giant could be defeated through a faith-filled heart and confidence in God. As David was running toward the battlefield to bring his brothers lunch, 1 Samuel 17:22 says he "left his baggage in the care of the baggage keeper." The battlefield was no place to be weighed down with "baggage." Those limiting thoughts of insignificance had been overcome as David experienced the strength of his God when no one else was around. He realized who was on his side. *With God*, David knew he could do impossible things. This kind of heart was something God could not overlook. He sent His prophet Nathan to declare promises over David's life that we still marvel at today.

> Now go and say to my servant David, "This is what the Lord of Heaven's Armies has declared: I took you from tending sheep in the pasture and selected you to be the leader of my people Israel. I have been *with you* wherever you have gone, and I have destroyed all your enemies before your eyes. Now I will make your name as famous as anyone who has ever lived on the earth! . . . Furthermore, the Lord declares that he will make a house for you—a dynasty of kings! For when you die and are buried with your ancestors, I will raise up one of your descendants, your own offspring, and I will make his kingdom strong. . . . Your house and your kingdom will continue before me for all time and your throne will be secure forever." (2 Sam 7:8–16 emphasis added)

This amazing promise from God was an eternal covenant with David. David himself could never have ensured his dynasty would continue beyond him, but God could. Even this promise speaks of the voice of insignificance David had to overcome. It was God who took David from his father's pasture and set him on the throne of Israel. David was not the type to hide in the baggage like Saul. He took his sins in prayer and worship before the Lord. It was the desire of David's heart to be found pleasing in the sight of God.

But remember this promise was not originally meant to be David's. God had wanted to give it to Saul. Saul's disobedience to the commands of the Lord, rooted in the belief in his own insignificance, kept him from receiving what God wanted to give him. In 1 Samuel 13:13–14, Samuel tells Saul,

> You have not kept the command the Lord your God gave you. Had you kept it, the Lord would have established your kingdom over Israel forever. But now your kingdom must end, for the Lord has sought out a man after His own heart. The Lord has already appointed him to be the leader of His people because you have not kept the Lord's command.

The cost of holding on to insignificance is greater than we could imagine. What if Saul had believed in who God wanted him to be? What if he had learned to walk *with God?* We would have read about all his amazing conquests. We might have heard the song of his heart toward the God who brought him out of obscurity and gave him a throne. Perhaps we would have read about Saul's mighty men and the armies he led into one victory after another. His story would have ended with the ascension of his son, Jonathan, to carry on his legacy. Instead, his life tells a much different story.

The voice of insignificance is still speaking. Even those who appear bold and confident have to overcome this voice. Remember fear wants to steal your identity. Insignificance wants to steal your purpose and, ultimately, your legacy. It wants to keep you from believing what God wants for your life.

"You're a nobody," it says. "Nothing special or talented to see here. Just so ordinary. Who do you think you are to even try? God already has a thousand others who are so much better than you. Why would He need you?"

Does that voice sound familiar? What kind of lies has it spoken to you? What measures has it taken to keep you hidden in your own baggage, reminding you of the smallness of your life? But, what happens when "With God" steps onto the scene? Those lies can't hold any weight at all!

With God, everything you do has significance because it's done in obedience to His voice. It brings about *His* desires on the earth. Listening to the leading voice of the Holy Spirit, you partner, or co-labor, *with God*. What He says, you say. What He does, you do. Where He leads, you follow. Suddenly, insignificance does not have a place in your mind anymore. You are about your Father's business, partnering *with God*. Your life is more significant than you could even dream possible. As 2 Corinthians 6:11–13 in *The Message* affirms:

I can't tell you how much I long for you to enter this wide-open, spacious life. We didn't fence you in. The smallness you feel comes from within you. Your lives aren't small, but you're living them in a small way. I'm speaking as plainly as I can and with great affection. Open up your lives. Live openly and expansively!

Know the Voice

REFLECT

- Looking over your life, what has insignificance tried to steal from you?
- What is the "baggage" in your life that insignificance wants you to stay hidden behind?
- What will it take for you to step out from behind that "baggage" and into the position of authority God is calling you to?

REMEMBER

- Marianne Williamson said, "Our deepest fear is not that we are inadequate. Our deepest fear is that we are powerful beyond measure. It is our light, not our darkness that most frightens us. We ask ourselves, 'Who am I to be brilliant, gorgeous, talented, fabulous?' Actually, who are you not to be? You are a child of God. Your playing small does not serve the world."[1]

RESPOND

Father God,

Help me to see myself the way You see me—free from insignificance and fear. Help me to see the potential You've placed within me. I want to believe with all my heart that, with You, there is nothing impossible. I want to believe every dream You've placed within me is possible because You are with me. How can I thank You enough for overcoming the enemy of insignificance and for entrusting me with Your dreams and purposes? I want to give everything I am to You. Every part of my life is Yours. Amen.

CHAPTER FIVE

Silence Insecurity

It's hard to live openly when you feel insecure. Perhaps you've heard someone say, "Your mind is a battlefield." Fear and insignificance have fought to gain control over your thoughts. The damage they have left behind is where insecurity comes in. It is the afterglow of this evil party, except no one is glowing.

All of us have encountered insecurity from two very distinct perspectives: within ourselves and in others. We have been the victim of insecurity manifesting in someone around us, and we have allowed insecurity to work through us. Insecurity is hidden in the taunts of a bully and in the shameful regrets of young ladies. It's beneath the mask of the most popular girl in school and maybe not-so-hidden in the overlooked, quiet girl you might pass by every day.

Insecurity is everywhere, but have you ever tried to define it? What is insecurity? And why are we so defeated by this enemy?

Let's go back to grammar class for a moment. You may remember the prefix *in-* means *without,* so a basic definition of insecurity would simply be *without security.* It's amazing how the lack of security turns into many different expressions in our behavior. One woman might assume dominance and lash out against anyone who gets in her way while another might shrink back into the background, hoping never to be seen. Both ladies may be dealing with insecurity internally even though how it affects them looks completely different on the outside.

Maybe one reason insecurity looks so different from one person to another is because we all have lived such unique lives. Our experiences, our personalities, the decisions we've made, all our quirks—they add up to the women we are. The sum total of your experience, personality, and peculiarities make you—*you*—sitting where you are reading these words right now. Every one of us has experienced hurt so deep we can barely speak of it, and all of us have experienced ecstatic moments of joy and love. I'd like to propose that those moments of pain—beginning when you were too young to realize you were hurting—are the source of your insecurity. Insecurity entered your life the moment you knew things were not what you thought they were or hoped they would be.

Remember Proverbs 13:12? It says, "Hope deferred makes the heart sick." You had an expectation—a hope—that was left there, unfulfilled or broken entirely, and it made your heart sick. Perhaps it was the divorce of your parents or the abandonment you felt when your mother left. Maybe it was when you were made fun of during gym class or when your father came home drunk in the evenings. Insecurity came in when what you had hoped for or expected, the security you were depending on, was suddenly gone.

Now, I realize how deep we just got. Maybe you felt guarded, vulnerable, or exposed as you read those words. More than likely, my words have reminded you of the experiences you would much rather forget! The problem is you haven't forgotten them, and I'm not sure you were supposed to forget them. We should not have to pretend the painful or difficult experiences were never a part of our lives. We should instead allow the Holy Spirit access to do what only He can do—heal our hurt, provide a balm to soothe us, and restore our security. So, my question for you is are you ready to give the Holy Spirit access into the deepest, most painful areas in your heart? Are you willing to expose the root system of insecurity in your life so that you become free from it once and for all?

I know these are daunting questions, considering the stories we have either lived out ourselves or heard about from others around us. But I also know the nature of the God we serve. He is a restorer. He is a healer. He is all-powerful. There is no story too complex for Him to comprehend. There is no heart too hard for Him to make new. And there is no brokenness that He cannot mend. He can reach you no matter how far away you feel you are. Most importantly, He cares about those moments from your past—those painful memories—and He wants to heal you.

Surprise Packages

When I was in my first years of college, I was surprisingly confronted by the emotional pain in my own heart. I was suddenly reeling in emotions related to my parents' divorce, feeling waves of rejection and doubt, and trying to figure out where all of it was coming from. It seemed there were things I could not remember—like my mind had somehow blocked them out to protect me. Pain seemed to be coming at me from every direction, and my emotions were in a tailspin. Here is an entry in one of my journals from that season to help describe what I was feeling:

> *Stability is lost, but I'm still striving, searching for what doesn't want to be found. The silence of yesterday drowns out the hope of today, stealing a moment of beauty and replacing it with pain.*

Stability is an interesting word to use. It is, after all, synonymous with security. My stability —my security—was suddenly gone. But why *then*? Why was I experiencing these emotions so far removed from the event they were associated with? It had been years since my parents had divorced. And why all of a sudden?

To answer those questions, I have to recommend a movie for you to watch. It's a pretty unlikely source of understanding why my security was at a sudden loss, but the movie does demonstrate how our emotions launch a surprise attack the way they do. The movie is *Inside Out*.[1] Riley, a young girl whose parents relocated their family to another city, is processing through the emotions of adolescence while struggling with being in a new school and away from her old friends. We get a look into Riley's emotions—Joy, Sadness, Fear, Disgust, and Anger—as they fight for control over her personality and actions.

Things really begin to get out of hand when the personified emotion Sadness begins picking up memories off the shelf of Riley's brain and changing them from joyful memories into sad ones. The emotions have to learn to work together to keep Riley from making some destructive life choices. Even though the movie features a hilarious cast of cartoon characters, the filmmakers consulted psychologists and medical specialists so the movie would tell more than simply a fun story. The film actually helps us better understand the emotions we feel and where they come from.

Looking back at my early college years, I can relate to Riley in a way. Memories I had lost or wanted to forget were suddenly before me. For whatever reason, Sadness picked up some memories from my brain's shelf. The emotions were real, and the hurt was deep. The disappointments I had experienced while I was too young to process them had been stored away to be dealt with when my brain felt ready for them. College was that time for me.

Like Riley, something dramatic like a physical move may trigger this clean-out process, or perhaps it begins as a tidying up of your own emotions. For one reason or another, the memory is before you, and you are processing the emotions like the hurt or injury happened only moments ago. It was all triggered for me at college when my boyfriend and I broke up. I thought we would be married and—as it turned out—I was right! My boyfriend was Samuel Bentley, now my husband. It just took another couple of years to get to that point.

When we broke up, my emotions tripped, and a lifetime of pain was before me. At that point in my life, my parents' divorce was almost ten years old. Surely it had been healed by then, I thought! But, no, the memory had been pulled off the shelf. The box was opened. What my brain had stored away to be processed at a later time was staring me down. It was time to confront the instability from that season.

The Gothic Months

My emotions were in a tailspin, and I didn't know how to process everything. One day, I decided to dress in gothic clothes as an experiment to help write a drama for Chosen, the Ramp's ministry team (I talk more about this team in Chapter 9). Strange, I know, but after a few failed attempts at writing a drama that was relevant to where people were, we were desperate to get the message right. The year was 2004, and gothic clothing made a statement that went something like, "I'm seething with anger inside. Stay away unless you're mad at life, too." We wrote the drama to Evanescence's song, "Bring Me to Life," that night, and I played the lead role of a young girl who ended up cutting herself to deal with the hurt she experienced. I didn't realize how much dressing the part would impact me.

The black nail polish seeped into my heart and became a dark comfort to me. My mom saw the effect the role was having on my spiritual condition and pulled it from our services until the spiritual battle was over. It lasted about three months, and during that time, I fell into depression. My Chemistry II grade went from an A to an F. School was no longer important. I felt so much anger. The only thing that brought any comfort was either creating some kind of art or writing a poem that could describe the turmoil in my head.

Thank God, my mother wasn't the only one to recognize something was going on in my life. There was another leader in my life who saw where I was. She encouraged me to write out as much as I could remember that had been painful through my life and bring it to her. When I brought her the pages of my pain written on notebook paper, I thought she would read them, feel desperately sorry for me, cry with me, then symbolically destroy them. She didn't do that at all. She didn't read one word—not one! As she told me that day, they were not for her; they were for me to present to my Heavenly Father. And that's what I did. I gave Him all that I had written on the pages in front of me. I had to trust Him with all my pain. Sitting in her living room that afternoon, I began to realize how easily I could overcome the darkness that was trying to overtake me.

Learning to Trust

In Mark 4, the disciples found themselves in a violent storm in the middle of a lake. They were absolutely terrified and thought they were about to die. That's when they ran to find Jesus asleep in the stern of the boat. "So they shook Him awake, saying, 'Teacher, don't you even care that we are all about to die!" (v. 38).

Jesus awoke, rebuked the storm, and commanded it to calm down. Instantly, the wind stopped, and the storm was over. Jesus then turned to His disciples and said, "Why are you so afraid? Haven't you learned to trust yet?" (v. 40).

Our raging emotions can feel very much like a storm that is determined to take us under its commanding waves. Those are the moments we find ourselves asking Jesus the same questions the disciples asked in their storm:

- Do You see what I am going through?
- Do You care about me?
- Are You there?

The truth is Jesus came when He was called upon. As long as the disciples were trying to ride out the highs and lows of each wave, working hard to steady the ship in their own strength, and cowering in fear with each gust of wind, Jesus remained fast asleep on their boat. But the moment they looked to Him, He didn't delay. He stood up, fully awake, and rebuked the storm. He did care. He was there. He just wondered why His disciples had not trusted Him all along. Why had it taken them so long to realize who was on the boat with them? If He was who He said He was, were they ever in real danger? Jesus spoke to their storm, and instantly the winds were stilled and their stability was reestablished.

Trust is a weapon we must use to confront insecurity. Have there been times of deep hurt in your life when you felt abandoned? Perhaps you felt there was no one there to protect you—no one who cared about the storm you were living in. Maybe it's difficult to imagine trusting anyone in that painful memory. This is a moment we must have supernatural strength. We have to call upon the One in the boat with us. This is the moment we need the Holy Spirit to reveal truth to us.

I want to invite you to ask Him a very powerful question that can dispel the lie insecurity has wanted you to believe. Take a prayerful, listening stance of your heart and mind. Then ask the Holy Spirit to reveal to you where Jesus was during that moment of your deepest hurt. And then, listen. Quietly and still. Just listen.[2]

If you will allow me to be completely vulnerable, I will share one of my moments with you. I was a month shy of twelve years of age. A few days before, my mom had told my sister and me that her marriage to my father was over. Before that, I never realized their marriage was in any trouble. She had sheltered us from the pain of it as much as she possibly could. My sister and I were standing in our living room. Dad's suitcase sat beside the hunter green chair he was waiting in. He was leaving our home forever.

71

It's the moment of the deepest pain in my heart. As I approached this moment during a prayer session with an intercessor friend, she asked me to trust the Holy Spirit with that same request: reveal where Jesus was in that moment.

For years, this memory always played out exactly as it had happened—the image of the hunter green chair and the suitcase, the emptiness I felt as my father walked out the front door and down the sidewalk, and me standing in the living room with my sister, holding onto mom as he drove away. When I trusted the Holy Spirit with this memory, I saw Jesus in the moment with me. He was there, sitting in the chair beside my dad. He embraced me as I cried. He was with me even though I had believed for so long that I was alone in that pain.

Maybe your own moments of pain bring on an emotional storm. Perhaps you find yourself fighting the waves, cowering in fear, and shaking from the intensity of the wind. Have you believed the same lies the disciples believed in their storm?

My friend, it is time to call on Jesus. This storm is trying to overtake you, and you need to be rescued. You need a Savior. It's time to open your heart and trust that He is on the boat with you, and that He *always* has been there. There's never been one moment you were left to deal with the storm alone. He was there in that most painful moment, and He is there with you now. The emotional storm you have fought is stilled at the sound of His voice. He has something to say about this moment in your life and

His presence in it. Most importantly, He *wants* to show you where He was and how much He truly does care.

Reforming Your Mind

I recently came across the lyrics to "Stressed Out" by Twenty One Pilots.[3] I was amazed as I read such a clear description of insecurity as the lyrics address the writer's being caught up in what others think, desiring to do better and be better. The last time I checked on YouTube, this video had 1.6 billion views! I'd say it's a song people relate to.

The truth is insecurity sings this song over all of us. And just like its co-conspirator, fear, insecurity wants your identity. It wants to blur your face out and keep you hidden. It wants to lock you up in regret. It wants you to care about what people think so you don't make the impact you were created to make. That's right, insecurity has teamed up with fear and insignificance to be sure the *you* you were meant to be never makes it.

One weapon insecurity uses is comparison. That's mentioned in the song by Twenty One Pilots. From comparing the sound of your voice to comparing your life against all the epic Instagram posts you follow, insecurity is communicating a very specific message: "You are not measuring up. You are not good enough. You probably never will be."

In 1990, a study was conducted on the rate at which our inner voice speaks. It was determined we can speak up to four thousand words per minute—that is ten times the rate for verbal or "out-loud" communication![4] Our inner voice is in constant communication with ourselves. What that voice is saying is shaping the person you are today. If insecurity has the reins, it is making sure you focus on the imperfections in your life, the flaws in your body, and the failures you may have experienced. It takes intention to recognize these patterns of thought and to break this cycle. Romans 12:2 encourages you to "stop imitating the ideals and opinions of the culture around you, but be inwardly transformed by the Holy Spirit through a total reformation of how you think. This will empower you to discern God's will as you live a beautiful life, satisfying and perfect in his eyes" (TPT).

The good news of the gospel is that Christ did for us what we could not do for ourselves when He paved the way to eternity with our Father. This good news continues to grow stronger in our lives when we choose to walk with the Holy Spirit, entrusting everything—even the thoughts we think—to Him.

The verse in Romans 12 says those thoughts in our minds every day can experience a total reformation! We don't have to listen to the voice of insecurity telling us all the things we will never be good enough for. A mind transformed by the Holy Spirit empowers you to conquer those lies. God has not planned a life for you that is full of disillusionment, abandonment, or emptiness. Jeremiah 29:11 says His purpose will give you hope. The life He has designed is just what Romans 12 says it is: a beautiful, satisfying life—a life that is perfect in God's eyes because He designed it especially for you.

The next time you catch your thoughts drifting toward insecurity, invite the Holy Spirit to take over right in that moment. If you are not sure what voice is speaking to you, remember the Holy Spirit will always speak words of wisdom, understanding, and peace. A condemning voice of fear, belittling, or insignificance is clearly the voice of an enemy. Darkness hates the light of God's truth. That battle between darkness and light is won when your trust is placed in the Holy Spirit, believing what God's Word says about you instead of what insecurity wants you to believe.

If you find yourself in a battle with insecurity, you need to build up an arsenal of truths from God's Word that dispels every lie this enemy wants you to believe. If the lie is that the dream God has put in your heart is too big and impossible to achieve, a truth from God's Word is that nothing is impossible with Him! If the lie in your mind is that you are stupid and can't understand spiritual truths, read this truth from 1 Corinthians 2:12, "And God has actually given us His Spirit (not the world's spirit) so we can know the wonderful things God has freely given us."

That inner voice of insecurity can be vicious, but God has something to say for each and every lie that voice would have us to believe. He has even equipped us with the Holy Spirit to search out truths in His Word that counter insecurity's lies. The storm insecurity creates in your mind is immediately stilled at God's Word. "Peace!" declares your God. "Be still," and the storm obeys. As it is written, "But the one who always listens to me will live undisturbed in a heavenly peace. Free from fear, confident and courageous, you will rest unafraid and sheltered from the storms of life" (Prov 1:33 TPT).

Know the Voice

REFLECT

- How has insecurity manifested itself in your life?
- What circumstances have you faced that "rocked the boat" and invited insecurity to enter your mind?
- Take some time to identify the lies insecurity has wanted you to believe about yourself. Look for verses in the Bible that combat these lies with God's truth. Begin to declare these verses over yourself. You can write them on index cards or sticky notes and post them on your mirror, keep them in your Bible, or display them somewhere so you can read them every day.

REMEMBER

- Trust is a weapon we must use to confront insecurity.
- Jesus has not abandoned you to face the hurts of life alone. He is right there with you. And He always has been.

RESPOND

Father God,

Every word You have spoken is true. You have never left me or abandoned me—even when I felt the most alone. Thank You for revealing where You were in the darkest moments of my life. I recognize my security can only be found in You. You are trustworthy, and I choose to open my heart and trust You completely. There is nothing off limits to You, no place in my heart You cannot see. There's nothing I want to hold back from You. All of my hope is placed in Your hands. When I feel afraid again, help me to remember You are right there with me. I trust You. Amen.

Part Two:
Hello, Lady

Returning to Confidence and God's Idea of Beauty and Purity

"Now it's time to be made new by every revelation that's been given to you. And to be transformed as you embrace the glorious Christ-within as your new life and live in union with him! For God has re-created you all over again in his perfect righteousness, and you now belong to him in the realm of true holiness."

—Eph 4:23–24

CHAPTER SIX

Redefine Beauty

We've come to a wonderful place in our journey. Let's take a moment to look back over where we have come from. Fear wanted to control your destiny and keep you hidden. It has been exposed! Insignificance wanted you to believe you didn't have anything to give. It has been silenced! Insecurity wanted you to believe you were too broken to be healed. It has been defeated!

It is my hope and prayer that fear, insignificance, and insecurity no longer feel like unconquerable enemies to you. Every victory over one of these enemies is worth celebrating. The battlefields you have fought on for years have been turned into dance floors! My friend, it is time to put on your dancing shoes and celebrate what God has won for you—how much He has done!

Now that we have released fear, insignificance, and insecurity to our Father, it is time to allow Him to restore His truth in our hearts. As we continue our journey, He has created a beautiful road for us to walk down, full of His love and purpose. He wants to restore beauty, purity, and confidence in His daughters. If you're ready, we'll make this turn together.

God Values Beauty

Have you ever noticed how much God loves beauty? Take a few minutes to look at a starry evening sky and feel the deep sense of awe that awakens in you. Spend an early morning in front of an ocean view or get lost in thought at the wonder of a rose growing in your backyard. When our eyes look upon beauty, there's something of the nature of God that draws us toward it. God is speaking to us in the beauty of art and architecture, mountains and oceans, people and their individuality.

Beauty seems to be important to God; in fact, I believe it's one of His core values as it is made visible in everything He touches. And this beauty has a power that speaks to our human heart, assuring us of His existence. As Psalm 19:1–4 says,

The heavens proclaim the glory of God. The skies display His craftsmanship. Day after day they continue to speak; night after night they make him known. They speak without a sound or word; their voice is never heard. Yet their message has gone throughout the earth, and their words to all the world.

We get a sense of who God is by looking at the world He has created. The beauty we see around us points to the One who created it just as a work of art reveals the heart, mind, and emotions of the artist. When we see the sunset and the stars, we observe the great worth God has placed in beauty. That beauty is constantly speaking to us of who God is—even though it's not using a voice.

A Different Kind of Beauty

There is a God-kind of beauty that is different from man-made beauty. The beauty of the ocean and the stars transcends our own human capacity to comprehend them. As we stand beholding the God-kind of beauty, fresh air filling our lungs and our very beings refreshed by the moment, we know a man's hand could not create such beauty. It is truly divine.

In the same sense, there is a God-kind of love, a beautiful love, that stands apart from our own human capability to love. In John 13:34–35, Jesus said, "So now I am giving you a new commandment: Love each other. Just as I have loved you, you should love each other. Your love for one another will prove to the world that you are my disciples."

People all over the world, believers and non-believers alike, experience love. They fall in love and are married. They love their children and have meaningful relationships with their families and friends. But there is obviously something that goes beyond our simple definition of love because Jesus has called us to love one another in a way that proves we are His disciples. This means our love for each other must look different from the love the world experiences. This difference is defined throughout the New Testament with directives like, "Love your enemies. Pray for those who persecute you," in Matthew 5:44, and in John 15:13, "There is no greater love than to lay down one's life for one's friends." First John 4:7–21 describes at length how important love is to the life of every believer. For example, verse 12 says, "No one has ever seen God. But if we love each other, God lives in us, and His love is brought to full expression in us."

While most people around the world are able to experience love, there is something supernatural in the love of a Christian. It is indeed otherworldly because it comes from God and it reveals who God is. God's love expressed through the lives of His children communicates His truth to the world: He is real, and He personally and individually loves those in the world. There is no one exempt from His overwhelming love. That's the message that is released by the power of the Holy Spirit when we walk in love.

God's divine beauty expressed through the lives of His disciples can have this impact as well. Godly beauty is a direct result of the work of the Holy Spirit in our lives. That kind of beauty becomes a fountain of life through which others can experience the love of God.

There is a beauty the world experiences—not only in the natural landscape around us, but also in our physical bodies. That's right! *You*, my friend, are beautiful. When Creator God looks upon you, He sees an expression of the kind of beauty only He can create.

You were created by the hands of this Master Artist. Each of His artworks is a masterpiece of beauty. Similar to love, there are people who exploit their physical beauty and use it for their own sensual impulses and selfish ambitions. They may feel confident in their outward appearance; however, they miss the power kept within in God's divine source of beauty—the power hidden in a gentle and quiet spirit.

The Road to Beauty

First Peter 3:3–4 says,

> Don't be concerned about the outward beauty of fancy hairstyles, expensive jewelry, or beautiful clothes. You should clothe yourselves instead with the beauty that comes from within, the unfading beauty of a gentle and quiet spirit, which is so precious to God.

No matter how confident someone is or how beautiful she is considered to be, there is another principle of beauty we should consider. External beauty fades away, of course. There is, however, an unfading beauty made available to us. As Peter says, it is the way of a gentle and quiet spirit.

I've heard this verse quoted time and again. It's easy to take those words at face value and believe God wants women to be calm, quiet, submissive, and lacking ambition. It seems God's definition of beauty would be outdated in our culture of women who operate in so many leadership roles. But we need to take a closer look at what Peter was saying because there's more to his admonition.

Rick Renner is a missionary to the nation of Russia. He has studied the Greek language extensively and has published several books that help Christians better understand the Greek meanings behind our English translations of the Bible. This passage in 1 Peter 3 carries so much more meaning than our English words, "gentle and quiet," can communicate. Rick Renner's book, *Sparkling Gems*, defines them this way:

> Gentle—the attitude of one who is friendly, warm, forbearing, patient, kind, and gentle. This would picture someone who is just the opposite of a person who is angry, temperamental, or given to outbursts of anger. Although a meek person faces opportunities to react in anger or to get upset, she has chosen to be controlled, forgiving, and gentle. Thus, meek people are individuals who have become skilled at controlling themselves and their temperament. You might say that meekness is power under control.

> Quiet—a person who knows how to calm herself and to maintain a state of peace and tranquility. Rather than speak up and utter words that are later regretted, this individual stays quiet and refrains from angry responses. She deliberately decides not to be a contributor to conflicts, but to be a peacemaker instead.[1]

There is so much depth to what Peter wanted to convey to Christian women in his day. He wanted them to learn control over their emotions and to be responsible for the environment they create. Paul knew women express all kinds of emotions—anger, envy, fear. He also recognized these emotions can set the atmosphere for what people around women experience. Women are atmosphere shifters. In the Deep South, we say it like this: "If mama ain't happy, ain't nobody happy." Women can set the tone of a room with just a facial expression or a sly comment. Left untamed, this gift can work against us. We can spread negativity and heaviness all around us.

The opportunity to unlock God's source of beauty is hidden within our own hearts. We must surrender this gift to the Lord and allow the Holy Spirit to teach us His ways. If you read over Renner's definitions of gentle and quiet, you'll notice they very closely resemble the fruit of the Spirit listed in Galatians 5: love, joy, peace, patience, kindness, goodness, faithfulness, gentleness, and self-control. When you open your heart to the leading of the Holy Spirit, you'll be amazed at how He gently corrects even the small opportunities we miss to make the right decision.

Runaway Driver

I was in Manchester, England, for a Ramp conference. When the ministry team members are there, we use public transportation and ride-share apps to get around because there's no way these American drivers are driving on the left side of the road! Most of the time, our ride-share drivers are very friendly, and even though Manchester is already a very diverse city, they are always intrigued by our Southern American accents. One particular ride, however, was different.

We had called for a van to get us around town. Our driver had a bad attitude from the moment some of our ministry team started getting into his van. We gave him the benefit of the doubt and rode toward our hotel in downtown Manchester, or as they call it, *city centre*. The ride was mostly quiet since the driver was obviously not interested in engaging in much conversation. As we approached the hotel, he missed his turn and rather than taking the loop to come back around, he threw the car into park in the middle of the road and told us the ride was over. It was a rainy night, and cars were swerving around our parked car. Immediately, I felt the need to take over the situation and assure him we would not be leaving the car until we had arrived safely at our destination. This did not faze him. He insisted the ride was over, and we were to leave his vehicle. Well, this did not faze me either. I sat fixed in the back row of the van, refusing to leave. After all, my name does mean victorious woman, right?

The driver and I went back and forth a good bit before my mom began gathering her things and telling us all to forget it. I was the last to exit his van and threw in a sharp, "One star for you. One! Star!" before closing the door loudly behind me and hurrying to the other side of the road. (Okay, slamming the door. I definitely slammed the door.)

We gathered in the hotel lobby for a few minutes to try and find some humor in what had happened only moments before. I think some of the team members were surprised to see me respond so strongly. I may not be as shy as I used to be, but I am typically calm—strong-willed—but calm. If it had been left up to me, I would have sat there for a good while longer. Thinking back, that could have had a not-so-safe ending, so I'm thankful someone else was there to pull me out of stubbornness and into reality. After all, being the driver, he did have more power in that moment than I did.

When I got back to my hotel room, I pulled out my laptop and began to prepare for the upcoming Reinvent class that I teach to young girls at the Ramp School of Ministry. As if it had been strategically planned, the session I was working on was this particular message on beauty. I was typing out the meanings of gentle and quiet. By the time I got to, "This would picture someone who is just the opposite of a person who is angry, temperamental, or given to outbursts of anger," I stopped typing, closed my eyes, and recognized the Holy Spirit was letting me know I had missed a good opportunity to respond in a godly way. I repented to the Father for not having maintained a quiet spirit and received His forgiveness and love. Sometimes, it takes situations as obvious as that to get us to see the ugly in our own hearts. As my husband likes to put it, "When someone bumps your tree, what fruit falls off?"

24-Hour Surveillance

The book of Proverbs is filled with examples of these little nudges the Holy Spirit will use to keep you on the right path toward a gentle and quiet spirit. For example, Proverbs 29:11 says, "Fools vent their anger, but the wise quietly hold it back." How many times do we call our girlfriends and use these exact words: "Ugh, I just had to vent to somebody"? This is not the way God wants us to respond. When we vent our anger, we share our offense with someone else. Proverbs 26:17 says, "It's better to grab a mad dog by its ears than to meddle and interfere in a quarrel that's none of your business" (TPT).

What seems like a small venting session that may feel relieving in the moment is actually exposing you and your friend to the bitter poison of offense. When we choose to take our situations to prayer or to a spiritual leader instead of making sure the situations make their rounds to all our peers, we find a different perspective awaiting us. Prayer and godly counsel can give us the wisdom we need to respond rightly. It takes maturity to step out of the emotions of the moment and choose the gentle and quiet road. Even the smallest victory in self-control is worth celebrating!

My mom had a situation arise that involved another Christian. The individual made false claims against her character. She spoke with a friend, who was a pastor, to ask for godly counsel in how to deal with this situation. You'll notice this is much different than venting anger. A Christian leader in your life—like a pastor, older family member, or friend—can see the bigger perspective and help you respond to difficult situations with wisdom. This pastor friend listened carefully to my mom's situation. He knew the claims this person was making were completely untrue; however, what the person had said still hurt because the individual had been a friend to my mom at one time. After mom spoke with her pastor friend, she called me to share a piece of his advice: "Karen, remember your life is under 24-hour surveillance by the Holy Spirit."

This is such a powerful truth to understand. Our lives—not just our actions, but our thoughts, motivations, and desires—are under 24-hour surveillance by the Holy Spirit. Even when we are truly the victim of someone else's mistakes, He is watching to see how we will respond. Will we call our friends to garner pity, or will we acknowledge God by inviting His counsel into the situation? He knows the beautiful woman you are called to be, and He will continue to chip away at anything that keeps you from becoming her.

The Goal of Our Lives

One of the greatest gifts in my life is my grandmother, whom I call Mama Nell. She does not recall a single instance when the sound of raised, angry voices filled her childhood home. I am the sixth generation of Spirit-filled women of God. While I'm thankful for this incredible godly heritage, I know it is rare and that many are believing for parents or other family members to be saved. Let this be a testimony to build your faith—that generations after you will remember the strength you walked in to set a bold example of godliness and beauty.

Mama Nell is a picture of godly beauty to me. She is gentle, full of wisdom and good counsel. I've never once seen her in an outburst of anger. Never once. She can diffuse any situation with peace. One of the most difficult seasons of her life was when my grandfather was diagnosed with Alzheimer's disease. He battled the illness for several years before suffering a series of seizures that left him bedfast for the last five years of his life. Every single day of those five years, my grandmother served him faithfully. His nurses were always amazed that he never developed bed sores. She was always there to see he was turned over and kept as comfortable as possible. We were all astonished she was able to lift him at all! My grandfather was an excellent football player and worked hard his entire life. He was unusually strong all the way to the end. Mama Nell always said the Holy Spirit gave her the strength to turn him and do everything she needed to do to take care of him.

When you have lived a life consistently responsive to the gentle nudges of the Holy Spirit's corrections, you will find His ultimate goal was to mold you into an image of godly beauty. People will be drawn to you because of the atmosphere of peace surrounding you. But this doesn't happen quickly. The kind of work He is doing in you takes many years of learning to recognize His voice and respond immediately in obedience to whatever He asks of you. My Mama Nell is the most beautiful woman in the world.

Dress-Up

You were made for beauty—but not only the external beauty that fades away. You were made for beauty that comes from the Holy Spirit living inside you. This kind of beauty grows more appealing the older you become as you grow more and more into the image of Jesus. As 2 Corinthians 3:18 says: "So all of us who have had that veil removed can see and reflect the glory of the Lord. And the Lord—who is the Spirit—makes us more and more like Him as we are changed into His glorious image."

Like most women, I love to feel beautiful and get dressed up for special events. I always have. Dress-up was one of my favorite things to do as a child. I could be a bride or a princess or a ballerina—all from my little collection of outfits my mom kept in a dress-up bin in the closet. But I'm concerned many of us don't grow out of this game. As women, we know how to look and play the part of someone who is strong. We can get what we want even if it hurts others in the process. We can post a picture that would seem like we think we're the most beautiful, confident woman, but inside, we feel the exact opposite. We know how to put on a façade and make people believe what we want them to believe about us. As my grandmother once told me, "You may hide an ugly heart with makeup and a great personality, but you are really only fooling yourself." First Samuel 17:7 says, "The Lord doesn't see things the way you see them. People judge by outward appearance, but the Lord looks at the heart."

Thankfully, that's why the Holy Spirit is here with us now. He wants to take those insecurities and the things we think of ourselves and change them to look like Jesus. This is the work of the Holy Spirit in our hearts. The beauty He creates out of a life that is devoted to Him is powerful! It brings strength to others instead of tearing them down. Godly beauty becomes a fountain of life for people to drink of the wisdom, peace, love, and joy that pour from Him through us! That kind of beauty reveals the truth of who God is to the world—that He is real and that He loves. It's the kind of beauty that only He can create. That beauty will never, ever fade away.

If you were sitting in my Reinvent class in the Ramp School of Ministry today, this moment would be a special memory we could share together. Although I may not be with you in person, the Holy Spirit *is* there with you. He is the one who makes this moment special. In today's Reinvent class, as the session would close, I would stand before you and a room full of other young ladies who have taken the journey to overcome fear, insignificance, and insecurity, and to redefine beauty. Each one of you have your own unique stories of what God has done in your hearts. We would take a little time to reflect on those victories, and then I would take a handful of makeup wipes and remove my makeup.

Leaving the box of wipes open, I would then invite you and the other ladies to join me in removing your makeup as well. We would use this moment to remove not only our makeup, but also every trace of the false identity the enemy has wanted to create in us through his lies.

You and I have reached a similar place in this book. God has brought us so far from the person we were, bound by fear and hidden behind insecurity and insignificance, to the person we are now. While there is always opportunity for growth on the road ahead, there is a lot to celebrate. Those enemies that once conquered us with darkness and kept us locked in shadows have been exposed. The light of the Holy Spirit has illuminated our hearts, and His truth has freed us. In this moment, we worship together, seeing ourselves the way God intended us to be—a radiant display of His divine beauty.

Know the Voice

REFLECT

- How does our culture's idea of beauty relate to God's idea of beauty in 1 Peter 3?
- Think of a woman you know who demonstrates godly beauty. Who is she, and what makes her beautiful?
- In a time of prayer, reflect back on the victories God has won in you over fear, insignificance, and insecurity. Take a moment to remove your makeup and stand before your Father just as He has made you, confident that He sees His divine beauty at work in your heart.

REMEMBER

- Your life is under 24-hour surveillance by the Holy Spirit.
- Godly beauty is a direct result of the work of the Holy Spirit in our lives. That kind of beauty becomes a fountain of life through which others can experience the love of God.

RESPOND

Father God,

Thank You for the gift of beauty. You have placed beauty all around us and let us experience who You are through it. I recognize that You care deeply about beauty. You desire the deep places of my heart to be yielded to the Holy Spirit so He can transform me into Your image. I give You permission to nudge me in the right direction when emotions get me off track. I want to be a channel through which other people can experience Your wisdom and love. Make me a yielded vessel to Your will. Amen.

CHAPTER SEVEN

Embrace Purity

Now, before you flip the page and skip this chapter, allow me to assure you of one thing. No matter where you are in your journey regarding sexual purity, I believe God wants to speak something to you. Every story is unique. Every experience is different. Perhaps you have never held a boy's hand before—much less kissed him. Or, maybe situations outside your control devastated you and robbed you of your innocence. Could it be that no one told you sex is something God created to be enjoyed within a marriage covenant and your virginity was lost before you realized what was happening?

Wherever you are and whatever your experience might be, I want to assure you I am not here to bring condemnation or shame. I believe the Holy Spirit can heal the deepest wounds. Furthermore, I'm convinced that every person can walk into the future with sexual purity! I'm asking you to trust me, but not just me. I'm asking you to trust the Holy Spirit, our Helper, our Friend. Trust Him even with this—the most personal and private area of your life. Trust Him—the Creator of all of this—with the decisions you have and will face regarding your sexual purity. He has something to say that will bring healing and hope, clarity and wisdom.

What Is Love?

You've probably heard of the Greek words for *love*. Sometimes, our English language fails us. Rather than specifying what type of love we're dealing with in any situation, we're just left with this one word: *love*. The New Testament was written in the Greek language, which used different words to describe the type of love being mentioned. For our purposes, let's look at two of the Greek words we interpret singly as *love*. This should help us have a better understanding of the kind of love we should desire in our relationships.

The first word is *eros*. It is sexual or sensual love. It is self-serving and not connected to commitment or a deep caring for another person. The other word is *agape*. This refers to the love God has for us and expects us to give to others. *Agape* recognizes the great value of love's recipient and honors that person to the point of sacrificing its own desires for the sake of the other person.

Did you know *eros*, or sexual love, does not appear one time in the New Testament—not even in the context of sex within marriage? The godly love we long to have in our marriages is not a self-serving, sensual love. The love a marriage must have to thrive is *agape* love. Look closely at the difference.

Agape love centers around the idea of value. It's a love that sees there is someone worth paying a high price for. The possessor of *agape* is willing to sacrifice time, energy, emotions—whatever!—to have the object of its love. It's the kind of love that's not just in the relationship to satisfy its own impulses, which are there one moment and gone the next. Instead of a self-serving, "take what I want no matter how it hurts someone else" attitude, *agape* love sacrifices its own desires to do what is best for the one it loves. It's the kind of love Jesus demonstrated for us, and it's the kind of love we *can* have in our marriages if we're willing to look and *wait* patiently for it.

My mother and my grandmother talked with me many times throughout my teenage years about a treasure God had placed inside me: my virginity. "It is like a beautiful diamond," they would say, "that belongs to your husband. Others will want to take it from you, but you must guard it." I knew, if I were to be a virgin when I walked down the aisle, it would be because I had taken the responsibility to guard that treasure with all of my heart. Because of their teaching me about the treasure I carried, I was a virgin on my wedding day. There were other lines I had crossed along the way, which I greatly regretted. I was not perfect, but I knew there was a reward in keeping my virginity for my husband. I believe part of that reward is in calling other girls and young women to a lifestyle of sexual purity.

The man I fell in love with and married, Samuel, had his own story with sexual purity. During his senior year of high school, his girlfriend became pregnant. Only a few months before the baby was born, Samuel was born again. He was discipled well, and by the time I fell in love with him, the sins of his past seemed like they belonged to another person altogether. He walked in sexual purity and honored his commitment to the Lord in our relationship. Although he had obviously lost his virginity before, he was able to walk into marriage with sexual purity. Why? Because purity and virginity are not the same thing.

Purity is your commitment to live according to God's desires. Samuel made a commitment to the Lord to do things His way, and Samuel held true to that commitment. I can tell you confidently that our marriage is one of God's greatest blessings in my life. Samuel's past sexual sins did not diminish his value to God. God paid the same price for the salvation of Samuel's soul as He paid for the salvation of mine or anyone else's.

Sexual sin does not change the value of your worth to God. Every one of your sins can be washed away, allowing you to stand before the Lord and the world as clean as if your life had never been marred by your sin.

What Am I Worth?

We misunderstand the heart of God when we believe sexual sin requires greater forgiveness from Him. If we believe this way, we believe our value has diminished because of sin. But that's not what determines your value.

First, let's think about what value means. Value is the cost someone is willing to pay in exchange for ownership. Let me give you this example. When the man of your dreams goes to the jewelry store to find the perfect diamond to propose with, the diamond itself does not determine how much it costs. Someone who has been well-trained to recognize the value of each diamond determines the price. God created you. He knows the great value He has placed in you, and He knew the great price of purchasing your eternal salvation. It cost Him more than we could ever fathom—His Son, Jesus. But to God, we were worth it!

Your value has been determined, and the price has been paid. You belong to God! So many young women have walked through Reinvent with heartbreaking stories of past sexual sins, rape, abortion, and prostitution. How my heart wants to hug every one of them and tell them their value to God is just as great as someone who has never had sex at all or someone who has never been violated! Value is not determined by what you have or haven't done, or by what's been done to you. Your value has been set, and the price has been paid. You were worth everything to God.

One young lady from Reinvent gave me permission to share her story here. She was committed to maintain her virginity and present it as a gift to the man she would marry on her wedding day. She had a boyfriend, however, who had been pressuring her to have sex with him for weeks, but she continued to resist him because of her commitment. One weekend, she went to a party at her friend's house. She finally gave in to him, and they had sex in one of the bedrooms. She was fourteen years old. When it was over, she looked up as he walked out the bedroom door and gave his friend a high-five. He'd taken what he wanted. She was left feeling worthless. He had taken something she felt she could never get back.

Throughout high school, she felt something was wrong with her. Her friends regularly slept with their boyfriends and didn't seem fazed by it at all. These friends even left gifts in the other girls' lockers when they lost their virginity. It was something they celebrated. But my friend felt nothing but brokenness on the inside.

By the time she graduated from college, she had no self-worth and tried to commit suicide several times. God spared her life each time. Years later, she finally hit rock bottom. She was an alcoholic who had tried drugs, been in rehab a few times, and done everything else she knew to heal her wounded heart. In a two-hour prayer meeting with some intercessory friends, God radically set her free. The week she was saved, she couldn't stop saying over and over, "God loves me!" God miraculously restored her life!

I had already been teaching Reinvent for some time when I first heard her story. She encouraged me to continue to tell young girls how valuable they are and what a treasure their virginity is. Looking back at her life, she knew that experience as a fourteen-year-old girl was the turning point for the years that followed. God did not let her story end in heartache. She made a commitment to purity and married a wonderful, godly man. They now share a life filled with hope and the restoration of everything she once felt was lost. The enemy's plan to steal, kill, and destroy her life was annihilated in one encounter with God's love and forgiveness. Her purity was restored, and she is walking confidently in God's purpose for her life.

God's Way

I know there are as many perspectives to this issue of sexual purity as there are individuals reading this book. We all have a story, and no one is perfect. Wherever you find yourself today, I want to invite you to walk in purity. Purity is the commitment to live according to God's plan for sex and intimacy. That plan is very clear: abstinence until you are married. That's it. Plain and simple. No frills or exceptions. God doesn't ask this of you because He wants to keep you from having fun. He wants to protect you from the heartache that comes when you share your body with someone outside the covenant of marriage. I have never known one person who regretted waiting until he or she was married to have sex. However, I have heard countless stories of girls who would do anything to be able to go back and change the decision they made to give up their virginity.

Our culture wants to make you believe losing your virginity is not a big deal—like it's just a part of life. That message is not backed up by the truth of God's Word. It *is* a big deal, and that decision carries major implications for your life. First Corinthians 6:16–20 in *The Message* speaks directly to this:

There's more to sex than mere skin on skin. Sex is as much spiritual mystery as physical fact. As written in Scripture, "The two become one." Since we want to become spiritually one with the Master, we must not pursue the kind of sex that avoids commitment and intimacy, leaving us more lonely than ever—the kind of sex that can never "become one." There is a sense in which sexual sins are different from all others. In sexual sin we violate the sacredness of our own bodies, these bodies that were made for God-given and God-modeled love, for "becoming one" with another. Or didn't you realize that your body is a sacred place, the place of the Holy Spirit? Don't you see that you can't live however you please, squandering what God paid such a high price for? The physical part of you is not some piece of property belonging to the spiritual part of you. God owns the whole works. So let people see God in and through your body.

Your heart may have broken when you read the words above. You may believe it is too late for you. Your virginity is gone, and you may feel there's nothing you can do to walk in purity again. I want to speak to you for just a moment. From reading the Bible, you'll find only one sin that is unforgivable, and sex before marriage is not it. You may not have kept your virginity before marriage, but you *can* walk into your marriage with purity. How? By making a covenant with God that, from this moment forward, your sexual behavior will be determined by His Word.

According to 1 Corinthians 6:9–11, you have been cleansed and made holy:

> Those who indulge in sexual sin, or who worship idols, or commit adultery, or practice homosexuality, or are thieves, or greedy people, or drunkards, or are abusive, or cheat people—none of these will inherit the Kingdom of God. Some of you were once like that. But you were cleansed; you were made holy; you were made right with God by calling on the name of the Lord Jesus Christ and by the Spirit of our God.

Did you catch what that verse said? Some of you were *once* like that, but you were cleansed! You were made holy! You have been made pure by the blood of Jesus. This verse says you are made right with God by calling on the name of Jesus. Hallelujah! Let those words take root in your heart today as you make a covenant with God to walk according to His will for your sexual life from this moment forward. You *will* walk into marriage with purity!

An Invitation to Purity

I want to invite you down a difficult road, the road of sexual purity. I know what it's like to be in the moment with a boy you like and have to ask him to stop touching you. It's not easy or fun, but it's worth it. You'll never once regret asking him to stop, but you will likely regret going too far.

This invitation is not only for the girls who've waited thus far to have sex; it's for everyone. Remember purity is not virginity. Purity is your commitment to live according to God's plan for sex. You can make that commitment today and walk into your marriage with sexual purity. Purity doesn't end on your wedding night. It's a daily decision to continue walking in purity, keeping to God's plan for sex. One man. After marriage. For your whole life.

During your single years, I would encourage you to have relationships in your life that can help you walk out this commitment. I'm talking about girl friends here! Find someone who has purposed to remain sexually pure and be strength to one another. It's not an easy road to walk down, so be sure you are armed with strength and good resources to help you reach your goal. You can do this. And you're going to be so thankful you waited.

Know the Voice

REFLECT

- List three sources that have shaped your views of sex, its purpose, its consequences, or its rewards. This may come from your first discovering what sex is, your first sexual encounter, movies, music, friends, or even school programs.

- How have those sources or experiences shaped your beliefs or decisions regarding sex?
- Are you ready to make the commitment to live according to God's design for sex?

REMEMBER

- Purity is not virginity.
- Value is not determined by what you have or haven't done, or by what's been done to you. Your value has been set, and the price has been paid. You were worth everything to God.
- Purity is the commitment you make to live according to God's plan for sex.

RESPOND

Father God,

I am making a commitment to You today to live according to Your plan for sex. I can trust that You have established boundaries because You know what is best for me. Father, wash me clean of every idea, desire, or experience that has shaped an unholy perspective of sex. I want to enter marriage with purity of heart and walk out my commitment to You for the rest of my life. Thank You for revealing the great worth You see in me. I choose today to value myself according to the value You have set for me. Amen.

CHAPTER EIGHT

Survive Dating

When I first began teaching Reinvent to the RSM students, I found most young, single girls are very interested in their future marriages. It has not been that long since I was young and single, and I remember the constant wondering in my heart, *Who is the one? Is it that random guy who just met my eyes in passing? Is he sitting right behind me in class, and I don't even realize it yet? Is it one of my guy friends? He could be anywhere!*

Now that I have some years of marriage behind me, it is a lot easier to sort out the emotions I was experiencing during those single years. "The marriage house" is a way I like to help explain what you might be feeling if you were anything like me.

What is *the marriage house*? This is the house that stands just down the road from where you live on your own, whispering daydreams of what marriage might be like. The windows are covered, and the door is locked, leaving you to pace the front porch wondering what . . . or *who* . . . might be waiting for you inside.

Your wedding, which you've probably been dreaming about since age five, is the front door of this house. You can decorate this door any way you want—cover it in extravagant white roses, rustic burlap and lace, or simply place a bouquet of lavender under the eaves. The front door is only the entrance into this beautiful marriage house, and as you're waiting on the front porch and occasionally looking through the tiny peephole, it only creates more questions than answers:

- What will your married life look like?
- What is your husband called to do, and how will your calling relate to that?
- How do you run a home? Have a family?
- What should you change to be more like the person you want to be for your husband?
- What is the rest of your life going to look like?
- Why has the man of your dreams not had a dream about you yet?
- What if you go on that missions trip at the same time your husband walks in the front doors of your church, and *you miss him*?!
- And for heaven's sake, who is on the other side of that door?!

We spend much of our single years stressing over all these questions and trying to make sense of the blurry images through the peephole. However, down the street, you live in a room of your own. If your time is spent stressing over the marriage house, your room is being neglected. Proving yourself faithful to steward your room will be greatly rewarded when the day finally comes and you are given charge over an entire house. If you neglect your room, you'll have a lot to learn when you are suddenly carrying the weight of an entire household.

Four Road Signs

I believe you are already taking time to steward your room well. Otherwise, you would not be this far along in this book! Letting go of fear, insignificance, and insecurity, and opening your heart to walk in sexual purity are huge victories! You are choosing wisdom, and according to the book of Proverbs, listening to wisdom comes with a long list of rewards.

There will be a day, however, when you fall in love with a wonderful, godly man. Whether you choose dating or courting or best friends turned more than friends, chances are you are going to fall in love. I want to share with you four road signs that can help keep you on the right path as you begin to make that move toward the marriage house.

ROAD SIGN #1: YOU ARE RESPONSIBLE

Many things may have impacted your perspective on sex, but those can't be used as an excuse to break your commitment to God. I want to share a piece of my own journey to let you know what I mean.

When I turned thirteen years old, an older family member took me to a lingerie store to pick out anything I wanted. Thankfully, I chose a modest pink satin bathrobe. I was too naive to even understand this was not a store for thirteen-year-olds. Not too long after this, this same family member sat me down to tell me to let him know when I became sexually active. He wanted to help me with birth control and condoms without my mother having to know.

Thankfully, my mother's and grandmother's influence was louder in my life than this person's. I never took him up on the offer, but I could easily have used this situation as an excuse for not honoring my commitment to God's plan for my life. I would have had to overcome so much hurt had I given in to this family member's offer.

Satan's plan is always for your destruction. God's plan is always for your best.

You are responsible for your own sexual purity. No one else. You can't depend on someone else to step into a moment of passion to stop you from going further. *You* have to draw the line. *You* are responsible. This does not mean the young man you are dating or are interested in isn't responsible for himself and his actions. He most definitely is; however, *you* are responsible for *you*, and you cannot expect him to do what is right regarding your purity. *You* do what's right anyway, and leave the young man to his responsibility for himself before God.

When I was a teenager, the purity slogan was, "If he loves me, he'll wait for me." Of course, I believe this is true. Real *agape* love is willing to wait for marriage. On the other hand, there is an aspect of this slogan that seems to put the responsibility for sexual purity on the man. It is not all on him, and it is not all on you. You both are accountable before God regarding how you treat each other. You must respect each other as children of God.

I am concerned when we take the idea expressed in the slogan into our relationships and put ourselves in situations that are almost impossible to escape with our sexual purity intact—and all in the name of "If he loves me, he'll wait for me." *Spirit-filled men are still men!* It's not right to dangle a carrot in front of a young man's face by the way you dress and carry yourself when you are dating. He is not now nor will he ever be perfect. If you flaunt your body in front of him to elicit a sexual response, you are no better than the woman called *Folly* in the book of Proverbs:

> *A woman of the night appeared, dressed to kill the strength of any man. She was decked out as a harlot, pursuing her amorous plan. Her voice was seductive, rebellious, and boisterous as she wandered far from what's right.* (7:10–11 TPT)

113

Your commitment to sexual purity is just that: It is your commitment. Of course, if the fellow interested in you really loves you, he'll wait for you; however, be sure you are not leaving the responsibility all on him. You are responsible to uphold the commitment you've made to live according to God's standards.

Before we move on, I want to clarify another thing. I recognize there are heartbreaking situations where sexual purity was taken without consent. While I personally don't have the experience to know the grief and shame you feel, I do know our God can heal the deepest of wounds and restore you. You can be made free and whole and continue to live out your commitment to the Father. Nothing can change the value He has placed on you, and there is nothing too hard for Him.

ROAD SIGN #2: LOVE SELFLESSLY

If we hope to receive the kind of selfless *agape* love we crave, we must be willing to give of ourselves selflessly in return. A man who truly values you will be thankful you draw the line and create physical boundaries for your relationship before marriage. That is loving him selflessly. It is saying, "No," to the things your body is demanding in the moment and choosing instead to say, "Yes," to what you know is best for both of you in the long run.

In moments like that, remember the difference between *eros* and *agape* love. *Eros* seeks to satisfy the carnal impulses it feels while *agape* recognizes the value of waiting.

You love selflessly when you choose modesty over seduction. It may make you feel more attractive to wear a revealing dress, but does that truly honor the man you love? If this is your husband, you will have plenty of opportunities to amaze him with the beauty of your body. But while you are still waiting to walk through the door of that marriage house, love him well by honoring and protecting his own covenant to his Lord to walk in sexual purity.

ROAD SIGN #3: DON'T SAY IT

There are two very simple ingredients to falling in love: time and vulnerability. How much time it takes may depend on the people involved, but vulnerability is a sure way to end up falling for someone. How many times have you found yourself liking someone after spending months insisting you are just friends? It happened because of time and vulnerability.

Those two things unlock the heart of a woman. We spend time with a guy. He's intriguing and fun. He's interested in who we are, so we begin to share our story. We tell him things we've never told anyone before. That communication opens the doors of our hearts to be vulnerable and let him see who we really are.

As the relationship grows, it's easy to throw words like "I love you" into the equation at the first opportunity. This is where I want to challenge you. Don't say those words unless you actually feel what *agape* love is toward him. *Agape* love is not the flighty emotions you will experience in your new relationship. *Agape* love speaks of a commitment, a value, a selfless love. Let's go back to that original Greek definition. Before you tell him you love him, be sure you esteem and value him.

Women thrive on emotion and language. That's why our hearts can't help but stir during the movie *Pride and Prejudice* when Mr. Darcy looks at Elizabeth and says, "You have bewitched me body and soul. And I love, I love, I love you. I wish from this day forth never to be parted from you."[1] How could a woman's heart not melt at that? I still don't understand her response to his beautiful confession. She takes his hands, and ends the conversation with, "Your hands are cold." But that's beside the point.

Words have power. Words are especially powerful to women. When we speak something, we want to act upon it. When we speak the words, "I love you," to a man, we want to demonstrate those words with action. We want to prove to him we mean them. This can put you in a situation you may not be ready for. Recognize the deeper meaning of those words. Hold onto them so that, when you are ready, they mean something when you say them.

ROAD SIGN #4: DEFINE YOUR BOUNDARIES

This may be the most important sign on the road to sexual purity. Do not wait for the heat of the moment to decide how far is too far. You can lay out your boundaries long before you're even in a relationship! You need to know where to draw the line. As we've already talked about, you have to take responsibility here. You can't expect someone else to step in and tell you where your boundary should be.

Set a high standard for yourself because God will give you His grace to keep to it. Even if you've gone too far physically in past relationships, don't let that be where you place your boundary line. Ask the Holy Spirit to help you know what the right thing is. If you're asking how far is too far, you're asking the wrong question. The Holy Spirit is very good at doing what He came to do. One reason He came to the earth was to convict us of sin. If you feel the nudge of the Holy Spirit, stop what you're doing and listen to what He tells you to do. Remember your life is under 24-hour surveillance by the Holy Spirit. He will help you know exactly where your boundaries should be—and even better—He will help you hold fast to them when you don't think you can.

So, remember these road signs as you are walking through the relationships that just may take you from your own room to the marriage house:

1. You are responsible for your commitment to sexual purity.
2. Love selflessly.
3. Don't say, "I love you," until you're ready to live what that statement means.
4. Define your physical boundaries before you find yourself in the heat of the moment.

Those Single Years

You may find yourself waiting for some time on the right man to come sweep you off your feet and carry you over the threshold of your marriage house. Those are precious years for you to discover more about who you are all on your own. Don't waste that time sitting around looking at every male as a potential spouse. That room of yours we talked about earlier could become Rapunzel's tower, where you're left wondering and wondering and wondering and wondering when your life will begin. Remember that song from *Tangled*?[2]

Your calling is not dependent on the man you marry to fulfill it; it's dependent on the God who called you to it! Use this time to explore your own interests and passions. What makes you feel alive? What makes you angry? Is there something you can do about it? Stepping out of your comfort zone to learn more about who God has created you to be just might place you in the *right* place at the *right* time for Mr. *Right* to come along. Okay, that was ridiculous. But I think you get what I mean. I mean don't wait to know who your husband is before you try to know who you are! Your life continues—not begins—the moment you get married.

There are those women who may feel called to remain single throughout their lives. If you feel called to singleness, even more so, establish a belief that your calling is not dependent on a man to fulfill it. If God called you to remain single, you can fulfill your purpose walking hand-in-hand with God.

You Can Be Powerful

Before we move on, I want to give you an early wedding gift to carry into your marriage house. As I've watched women take on stronger roles of authority and leadership, I've also seen something heartbreaking. So many of these women neglect their homes to pursue their dreams. The gift I want to give you is this truth: You can be a powerful woman without sacrificing your family.

The whole idea of lifelong love that we so long for is just that: *lifelong love.* We have as much responsibility in making that happen as our husbands do. Remember that whole thing about *agape*, selfless love? That means you, too. In your marriage. Every day. Long after the butterflies in your stomach move away, your love will remain steadfast and sure, built on the solid foundation of God's *agape*, selfless love. The key to your dream life with your dream man is found in simply loving your husband every day.

The passion you feel inside you to accomplish great things with your life is third in priority after your own personal walk with God and your family. Your family is your responsibility to steward well. Paul speaks very strongly about this in 1 Timothy 5:6 and 3:5. He says, "But those who won't care for their relatives, especially those in their own household, have denied the true faith. Such people are worse than unbelievers," and "If a man cannot manage his own household, how can he take care of God's church?" The example of the Proverbs 31 woman also speaks of a woman's responsibility to her home, "She carefully watches everything in her household and suffers nothing from laziness" (v. 27).

You will likely be given a home and family to steward. Be sure to keep them as your priority second only to your personal relationship to God. Fulfilling the dreams in your heart will be more satisfying to you when you are able to share them joyfully with your family. Remember this on the days it's hard to be only a wife and mother. Yes, it is a lot of work and responsibility; but even those days are tools in the hand of the Holy Spirit to shape you into who He's called you to be. You'll come out stronger and better able to accomplish even more for His Kingdom. I believe Proverbs 31:28–29 will be part of your reward: Your children will bless you, and your husband will praise you.

Know the Voice

REFLECT

- What kind of person would you like to spend your life with?
- What physical boundaries do you feel the Holy Spirit is comfortable with for your current or future dating relationships?
- What are some things you would like to do—some goals you would like to accomplish—before you get married?

REMEMBER

- The four road signs for your journey from the room of your own to the marriage house are:
    1. You are responsible for your commitment to sexual purity.
    2. Love selflessly.
    3. Don't say, "I love you," until you're ready to live what that statement means.
    4. Define your physical boundaries before you find yourself in the heat of the moment.
- Your calling is not dependent on the man you marry to fulfill it. It is dependent on the God who called you to it.

RESPOND

Father God,

Today, I am trusting You—just like You asked me to in Proverbs 3—to trust in You completely and not rely on my own opinions. I am trusting that You will guide every decision I make in my dating relationships. Give me strength to overcome the temptation to break my covenant with You. I want to enter my marriage with purity of heart and to live according to Your will. Your way is the best way for me. That's the way I choose to go. Amen.

CHAPTER NINE

Build Confidence

People have told me I come across as a confident woman. I wish I could laugh out loud at this without hurting their feelings. Even more, I wish I could let them inside my thoughts for a day. I have my own insecurities to battle. For ten years, I played the keyboard in our worship band, but I can't tell you how many times I ended up hiding after the set was over. If I had made a single mistake, all I wanted to do was crawl under a rock and die there. I felt embarrassed. Never mind the volume on my keyboard was turned down so low hardly anyone could hear if I was even playing the right chords. Whatever the opposite of confident is, that's what I was.

It's taken a lot of time and processing for me to feel confident about speaking in front of people or doing anything that involves letting a piece of myself be known. Through the years, I have come to find the lack of confidence is something almost everyone battles. There are times we feel great about ourselves and other times we feel we blew it completely. I have been amazed to see people I view as confident and bold from a ministry platform feel just as vulnerable backstage as I have been before.

I remember one time I had been asked to say something before the service started at the Ramp to a room full of people. As I was walking out, I felt the awkward moment coming on and knew I had no idea what to say to break the ice. I ended up saying something silly about the high-heeled shoes I was wearing. I blubbered out whatever it was I was supposed to say, then got ready to crawl under my rock and die a thousand deaths. That's the moment I realized no one else was going to spend longer than fifteen seconds reliving whatever I had said. It was just me. No one else has the time to dwell on your mistakes. If you say something embarrassing, it's okay. Just move on. Keep going. The lighter you make of it, the lighter it will be.

Even the most-confident-seeming lady in your life still looks in the mirror and wants some flaw to be perfected. Have you ever met a woman who was perfectly happy with her body? Neither have I. Everyone is able to recognize their own flaws. When we compare ourselves to the selfies our friends post, we get this never-measuring-up feeling that breaks down confidence.

Now, we've already discussed at length where godly beauty comes from. That internal beauty should also be the source of your confidence. When you know where your strength comes from, you carry yourself differently. Your approval is not found in the applause of men but in your relationship with the Father. When your confidence comes from being fully known and loved by your Father, it impacts the world around you. It's okay if you mess up and stumble over words. You can always practice to do better next time. If you make a mistake, you can pick yourself up and try again because you know the Holy Spirit is there to take you and lead you through it.

I love what the prophet Jeremiah said, "But blessed are those who trust in the Lord and have made the Lord their hope and confidence" (17:7). The Lord is our hope and our confidence!

Be Confident

Confidence is something we witness on the outside. It's the way people carry themselves. It's their manner or bearing. It can be heard in the way they speak or interact with others, but its source comes from their knowing who they are.

How you present yourself does matter. So many times, we appear on the outside the way we feel on the inside. When we're sure of ourselves, we walk with our shoulders back and our heads high. When we're fearful and embarrassed, we walk with our shoulders dropped and our heads down. We try to hide in the shadows and avoid eye contact.

When it comes to confidence, sometimes you have to start by playing the part. As long as you're walking hand-in-hand with the

Holy Spirit so you know the true Source of your confidence, why not just give it a try?

I took some acting classes in college. They were some of my favorite courses. One year, our final project was to interview someone from a different culture and deliver a monologue in front of the class, acting as that person. I chose to do my project on a Middle-Eastern man. Our teacher, Charlton, had instructed us to begin with our backs toward the audience and "become" the character before turning around to deliver the monologue. I wore my hair up in a makeshift turban that day. With my back turned to the audience, I pulled black eyeliner out of the pocket of my leather jacket to color in thick eyebrows without a mirror. I became the Middle-Eastern man, then turned around and delivered my monologue. I don't remember much about my speech, but I did get an A on that project.

Fear, insecurity, and the other issues we've talked about so far have kept the confident you from really being seen. Perhaps you don't know how to be confident—even if you no longer feel the fear you felt before. So ask yourself these questions: What does a confident woman look like to me? How does she walk? What does she do that communicates her confidence? Take notes on how she carries herself, and then give it a try! Get into character. Walk like she walks. Talk like she talks. You can practice at home before taking it out into the real world, if you like.

What does your voice sound like when you speak with boldness instead of intimidation? Let your own ears hear that sound of authority and confidence in your voice. Let it become part of who you are because that confidence *is* who you are!

Post the Silly

I love seeing people be real. We all do. But when it comes to letting people see the real us, well, that's a different story. Like lots of other shy girls, I always came alive when I was home. My sister, Lindsey, has a gift for pulling a smile out of the most serious of faces. She has always been one to enjoy the fun things of life. When we were younger, I was the most silly with her, but no one would have ever guessed it. I was far too serious to behave in such "demeaning" ways in public. It might hurt my precious reputation, or so I thought.

Something happened in me after God dealt with the stronghold of fear in my life. Suddenly, being known was not such a terrifying idea. I found ways to have fun and express the abundance of quirks in my personality—like the time I wore a Christmas tree tied to the top of my head to a dinner party or when I dressed up like a giant gingerbread man for a costume party. Never mind that the costume was made for a child and looked absolutely ridiculous. It was fun for the moment and something no one would have expected given my very serious personality. Those who are closest to me know I'm not *that* serious, anyway.

Then, I started posting some silly things here and there on social media and discovered that people want to connect to real people. There are plenty of people who always put their perfectly manicured feet forward, but that's just not real life. People relate to you the most when you're the most relatable. They want to see who you really are—quirks included!

Now, I'm not saying this to be disrespectful. There is a time and place for everything, and there are plenty of times when silliness is tasteless. But don't be afraid to put who you *really* are on display right there alongside all the glamorous, epic pictures everyone loves to post.

Different Strokes for Different Folks

I had not done much public speaking. Occasionally, I greeted people from the stage at the Ramp. I didn't have much confidence when it came to speaking. Given my position at the time, I was forced into different situations that required addressing groups of people. One night as I was preparing to say something over the microphone, someone told me I reminded them of a certain preacher's wife. She went on to say, "She's one of the worst public speakers I've heard." It was not exactly the boost of confidence I needed right before I took the stage. Thankfully, I shook off the comment and stayed focused on what I needed to do.

Less than a year later, I was in a business communications class in college. We had to deliver several speeches in front of the class throughout the year. My professor left her final reviews online for us. One of her remarks to me was that public speaking came naturally to me and she hoped I would do it for a living. I wanted to laugh out loud as I remembered the words spoken only a few months before.

At some point in your life, someone is going to find a way to put you down. You have a choice in that moment to let it become a part of your identity or to fight against it and do exactly what they thought you couldn't do. Just because your style of communication or singing or whatever expression you use doesn't fit someone's taste, it doesn't mean you should shut down a gift you feel God has given you. Sometimes, it's the areas we are the weakest in that God wants to give us the greatest victory. It will be our weakness that causes us to depend more heavily on His strength. If we're doing it all for Him anyway, does it really matter if we stand on a platform or if we sing in our bedroom?

Socially Awkward

You are socially awkward. It's true. So am I. Actually, everyone is. I get this comment from girls in Reinvent all the time, "I'm sorry. I'm just so socially awkward." What they are really saying is they lack confidence in themselves in that moment. They aren't sure what to say or if they can actually be themselves without ridicule.

We all come with personalities that are absolutely unique to us. There is truly no one else exactly like you in the world. Sure, there are personality profiles we can take. It's fascinating to see how personality works within those! One of my personal favorites is the Myers-Briggs test. You can take it for free at 16personalities.com. But, your personality type isn't the only thing that you are made of; otherwise, we'd live in a very boring and stereotypical world. It's all the little idiosyncrasies in your personality that set you apart as different from everyone else.

In Matthew 22:39, the Pharisees asked Jesus which commandment was the most important. Jesus replied, "You must love the Lord your God with all your heart, all your soul, and all your mind. This is the first and greatest commandment. A second is equally important: Love your neighbor as yourself." Before we can love other people well, we have to learn to love ourselves. If we don't love ourselves, we go into friendships looking for the approval of others to feel valuable. What we're really looking for can only be found in God.

That kind of confidence lets us see people the way He sees them—needing to experience His real love for them. Everyone has a story of feeling left out or belittled by someone. Those are not the times we look back and feel valuable. We feel embarrassed for having spoken up or ashamed that we put ourselves out there to be bitten so harshly by rejection. It's rare to find the kind of person—sadly, especially a woman—who is willing to put her own need for approval on the back burner to include someone who's trying to fit in. If you want to build confidence, be a confidence builder for others!

It is my prayer that as you read this book, the Holy Spirit is walking you through a journey of real life change—a journey that moves from the inside out and affects not only the way you think, but also the way you carry yourself. While your confidence is rooted in Father God, it is on display for others to see. When strongholds of fear, insignificance, and insecurity are peeled back, the *real* you is able to be seen. And she, my friend, is *stunning*.

Know the Voice

REFLECT

- Think of a woman in your life who you would perceive to be confident in a healthy way. How does she communicate that confidence to you?
- What areas in your life have you shut down because someone told you that you were not talented or good enough to do them?

REMEMBER

- "Blessed are those who trust in the Lord and have made the Lord their hope and confidence" (Jer 17:7).
- If you want to build confidence in yourself, be a confidence builder for someone else.

- The approval we so desperately seek from others can only be satisfied in the Father. That is where real confidence comes from.

RESPOND

Father God,

Thank You for being strong in the areas I feel the weakest. Help me to overcome the opinions of people around me and instead focus on obeying Your voice. I recognize my source of confidence must come from You, or it will never satisfy my heart. I choose today to make You my confidence. I am committing my strengths and my weaknesses as tools in Your hand to use as You see fit, regardless of what people around me may think. I want to always say yes to You, no matter what You require or ask of me. Always, always, yes! Amen.

CHAPTER TEN

Be a Friend

During a session of Reinvent, I asked the class of around fifty girls if they had found it hard to be friends with other girls and would rather befriend a boy. The girls laughed aloud as they looked around. Every girl in the room was holding up her hand. One girl even said to the class, "I thought I was the only one!" I went on to ask them why, and they were not short on answers:

- "Girls are mean."
- "They betray you."
- "So much emotional drama."
- "Girls are jealous."
- "They are friends to your face but talk about you behind your back."
- "They hold grudges."
- "They share your secrets."

As they continued sharing answers, it was obvious there was not a girl in the room who had lived without being wounded by someone she had once considered a friend. Sadly, these issues are part of the sinful nature of women. As much as we would like to claim the victim role in all of these scenarios, that is simply not the truth. We've all been guilty of these offenses toward our girl friends. We've lost friendships and hurt the beautiful women around us for one reason or another, or maybe without even realizing what we've done.

Where Two Agree

In Matthew 18:19–20 Jesus says, "I also tell you this: If two of you agree here on earth concerning anything you ask, my Father in heaven will do it for you. For where two or three gather together as my followers, I am there among them." No wonder the enemy fights friendships so hard! It's certainly not the easy road to repair broken relationships. It takes emotional work, admitting you were wrong, and facing the fear of trusting after you've been hurt. But there is power in walking through life with other believers.

When you feel wounded by a friend, it's difficult to imagine the hurt she may be experiencing because of something you did or didn't do. You may not even realize she's hurting! Of course, this is not always the case, but we must forgive others so we ourselves may be forgiven. Remember it is very likely you've been guilty of the very thing she has done to hurt you. The important thing is to be merciful and not defensive. James 2:3 tells us, "There will be no mercy for those who have not shown mercy to others. But if you have been merciful, God will be merciful when he judges you."

When I make mistakes, I expect God looks at my entire life to see the reason behind *why* I made such a foolish decision. Maybe the mistakes were made because of old hurts in my life or because the person hit a nerve with me she didn't realize ran so deep. It could be anything; but as the person in the wrong, I expect God will see all of those things and offer mercy. Oh, that I could see the person who wrongs me in this way!

Rather than seeing the woman who treats me with such spite, could I see instead the young girl who was raised by an alcoholic father and bitter mother? Could I have love awaken in my heart for her and treat her with the Father's love? Rather than seeing the woman who betrayed my trust and spread lies about me, could I see instead the girl who felt rejected, alone, and invisible? Rather than seeing the woman who puts me down in front of others and points out as many flaws as she can find, could I see instead the girl whose own father called her "Thunder Thighs" throughout her teenage years? Could I pray for the beauty that's inside her to be revealed?

If we want others to extend mercy and understanding to us in our mistakes, we must extend it to them in theirs. Praying from this perspective will change your heart toward them. People are hurting and need someone to break through their own need for approval to make room for someone else to feel loved and accepted.

Be that kind of friend. Love selflessly. You'll find you are a rare gift of friendship, and you'll be rewarded with friends who return that same kind of love to you.

Choosing the Right Friends

Take a minute to think of your closest friends. What draws you to them? Is it their style or personality? The interests you have in common?

Who your friends are says everything about who you are. Jim Rohn once said, "You are the average of the five people you spend the most time with."[1] They are the people you turn to when things don't go your way. They are the ones whose advice you are most likely to hear. Choose the right friends.

You'll know your friends by the fruit of their lives. What do you feel called to do? Rather than waste your college years trying to fit in with the crowd, what if you had two or three friends who—like you—felt their lives had significance to make an impact in a cause? The Holy Spirit will put people in your life to call you higher. They may not always be the most popular girls, but they will sharpen you to live a purpose-filled life.

The worst year of my life was 2015 when my only sister had left her family and filed for divorce.[2] The already strained relationship with my father was at an all-time low. My grandfather, who had been the kind of man every young girl needs in her life, was winding down his long fight with Alzheimer's disease. I lost friendships during that season of my life I thought would always be there. There were many dark days throughout that year—many days I didn't want to get out of bed and face reality. It seemed like the people I needed love from the most were intent on inflicting more pain in my heart.

The Holy Spirit is so near to the brokenhearted. It hurts desperately to lose friends and to feel alone. But the truth is you are never alone. My grandmother says it like this: "When I don't have someone there to agree with me, I just say, 'Holy Spirit, I agree with You.'"

Coming out of that season, God did some of the greatest miracles I have personally witnessed. My sister came home, and God fully restored her marriage. She and her husband, Casey, had a third miracle baby just eleven months later—my first nephew! Hallelujah!

Some of the lost relationships have not yet been restored; however, I came out of that season with such an appreciation for the work God did in my own heart. When you've been hurt, it can be hard to trust again. It would have been a far easier road to have just closed that door to vulnerability forever. Trust is scary. Love is scary. They both involve risk.

After 2015, I viewed friendship differently. I wanted to have people who sharpened me, people who called me up and into my purpose. I found friendship to be a precious gift from God we have to steward well. We have to forgive quickly and ask others for forgiveness. We have to love through hurt. We have to be the kind of friend we want others to be to us. There are plenty of faultfinders.

Be one who sees value in someone else and pulls that strength to the surface so they can shine.

The Ramp

One of the places where I have witnessed the closest friendships and how they can impact an individual's life and even the Kingdom of God is the Ramp. The Ramp first started as a youth group, probably like one you may have attended. We met in the back room of a storefront church. When my mom began working with the youth group, she developed Chosen. We were almost called *Comradz* because it was the early 2000s, and that was a thing. Let's take a moment to be thankful we landed at Chosen.

Chosen was never a team you could apply or audition for; it was more like an assignment. Mom would feel drawn toward a particular person. She would approach him or her with what it means to be a member of the team—like practice commitment, travel schedule, the commitment to live a Christian lifestyle without compromise. After prayerful consideration and talking it over with a young person's parents, the person would either accept her invitation or not. There were never more than thirty people on the team.

I spent all of my college years traveling with Chosen. We built so many amazing memories and had moments in the presence of God I still can't talk about without crying. We were a family—a very close group of friends—who shared a mission of awakening a generation to the God we had encountered. We traveled across the nation, calling people to live radically and passionately for Jesus.

Not everyone who joined Chosen stayed on the team. Some came for a few months before leaving for college or another career opportunity. Others stayed for many years and left to serve in a church or to build their families. Regardless of how long someone was on the team, they experienced the power of *unity*. Joining our lives with people around us in a singular mission for the Kingdom of God allowed us to tap into a supernatural synergy. We all want to be part of something that is bigger than ourselves. We want our lives to matter. This unity is the key for stepping into that significance in God's Kingdom.

When we were only a youth group who prayed together, we never imagined God had something like the Ramp in mind. We just wanted to reach our high school for Jesus. We wanted people saved. We came together to pray for the people we went to school with. That unity we shared opened doors for us we could have never done in our own strength. This is still the mission of the Ramp: to awaken a generation to the God we have encountered. We create an atmosphere that welcomes His Presence, and He is still faithful to come and transform lives.

Being on Chosen and experiencing all of these things had a huge impact on who I am today. I became an average of the people I surrounded myself with. We all do. That's why it is so important to choose your friends with intention. Don't just befriend the people it's easy to click with. Befriend the people who have the same core values and desires. Spend your time with those whose trajectory is pointed in the same direction you want to go. Your friends ultimately help determine the way you spend your time and what you choose to do with your life.

Know the Voice

REFLECT

- Think of a woman in your life who has consistently belittled or hurt you. What challenging circumstances in her own life might have led her to treat you the way she did? How does this change your perspective of her?
- What five people (outside your immediate family) do you spend the most time with? Are they reflective of the kind of person you aspire to become?

REMEMBER

- Jim Rohn said, "You are an average of the five people you spend the most time with."
- There are plenty of faultfinders. Be one who sees value in someone else and pulls that strength to the surface so they can shine.

RESPOND

Father God,

I am so thankful for every friendship You have given me. Help me to become the kind of friend who is not intimidated by the strength around me, but instead sharpened and encouraged to become stronger myself. Today, I choose to see friends who have hurt me from a different perspective—from Your perspective. Help me to go beyond my own need for acceptance and to love and forgive people who have hurt me. I want to be strength and encouragement to the women You've placed in my life. Heal my heart from any hurt that would keep me from loving them the way You do. Amen.

CHAPTER ELEVEN

Walk in Victory

What an exciting journey we have taken together! I know the issues we've discussed are no small things. Fear, insignificance, insecurity, wounds from the people around us—these are not easily confronted. They are, however, easily defeated when we realize the victory Jesus won for us.

Walking in victory is a daily decision we make. We can't think we deal one time with an enemy like fear and never have to face it again. How I wish that thing would leave us alone! But it doesn't. We have to choose faith *daily* over fear. Victory over defeat. Significance over insignificance. Confidence over insecurity. Forgiveness over holding a grudge. Trust me, you will get plenty of opportunities to make these decisions!

As you begin to walk these things out, I want to leave you with two foundational elements that will keep your eyes fixed and keep you walking straight toward your purpose.

A Woman of Prayer

The first is to be a woman of prayer. Prayer doesn't have to be scary or intimidating. It's just talking to your Father God. He already loves you completely. More eloquent words are not going to impress Him. He just wants to hear your voice.

In prayer, our minds have a tendency to wander, especially in a time where distractions abound and information is everywhere. We are accustomed to constantly diverting our attention and moving quickly from one thing to another or doing several things all at once. Prayer cannot be like that. This is the kind of prayer Jesus discouraged in Matthew 6: "When you pray, don't babble on and on as the Gentiles do. They think their prayers are answered merely by repeating their words again and again."

When we pray with our mouths but allow our minds to run with every passing thought, there is no real connection with the Father. And *that* is the central purpose of prayer: connection. When we engage our minds in the place of prayer, we open our hearts to experience His Presence. That connection with heaven gives you access to everything you need.

Praying from the heart means more than merely speaking words to God. It is expressing your own emotions and desires to the Father. It's just like sharing your day with your best friend. When something happens that makes me feel angry or upset, I immediately call my husband to replay the experience and share those emotions with him. Sometimes, I call my mom or my sister and tell them. It's what you do when you share life with someone. I tell them because I know they care about me. I tell them because they've proven trustworthy and can speak truth about how to handle those situations. God wants to be in that circle! Prayer is the place where you share those experiences and emotions with Him so He can reveal His wisdom, bring healing, and even pour joy into those moments.

The next time you are in prayer, pray from your heart. Don't try to be someone you're not. God loves connection with you—the *real* you—because it shows Him that you trust Him and it's through that connection you will get to know Him.

Dependence on the Holy Spirit

From the beginning of this book, I have emphasized our need to have the Holy Spirit actively involved in our lives. He is not some mystical, abstract idea. He is God, and He is *with* us. The Holy Spirit makes it possible to deal with the things we've talked about in this book. By processing through those issues, He is changing you into a beautiful reflection of Jesus—just as we read in 2 Corinthians 3:18.

> So all of us who have had that veil removed can see and reflect the glory of the Lord. And the Lord—who is the Spirit—makes us more and more like Him as we are changed into His glorious image.

The Holy Spirit partners with you to see the manifestation of Jesus through you. He can love others through you and release wisdom through your lips. All you have to do is know He is your source and allow Him to fill you. Father God *wants* to fill you with the Holy Spirit. He is not holding Him back. All you have to do is ask!

Jesus said,

> Let me ask you this: Do you know of any father who would give his son a snake on a plate when he asked for a serving of fish? Of course not! Do you know of any father who would give his daughter a spider when she had asked for an egg? Of course not! If imperfect parents know how to lovingly take care of their children and give them what they need, how much more will the perfect heavenly Father give the Holy Spirit's fullness when his children ask him. (Luke 11:11–13 TPT)

Some people have mistakenly believed the Holy Spirit opens the door to some kind of evil, but this verse addresses that specifically. If your heart is asking the Father to fill you with the Holy Spirit, He will not turn around and give you something evil in response—like a snake or spider. He is a perfect Father whose love is perfect. He knows you need the Holy Spirit, and that's why He wants you to ask for Him. The Holy Spirit wants to walk with you and do exactly what He's here to do: lead you into all truth. Walking in truth sets your heart free! As Jesus said, "When you continue to embrace all that I teach, you prove that you are my true followers. For if you embrace the truth, it will release more freedom into your lives" (John 8:31–32 TPT).

It really is as easy as asking the Holy Spirit to come and fill you, then believing in faith—as you did for salvation—that He has come! When we ask for forgiveness of sin, we believe we are forgiven. We trust the Father to forgive us, and we walk away with the faith to believe we've truly been made clean. Being filled with the Holy Spirit is also done by faith. We ask to be filled, and then we walk with the faith to believe He has filled us!

Victorious Woman

As our time together comes to a close, I'd like to stop and look back over this wonderful journey we've been on. Perhaps you began without knowing how much fear, insignificance, and insecurity had taken from you. Today, that ground has been reclaimed, and you stand in victory over these enemies. The girl you once were, who walked with her head down and her eyes low, now walks with a confidence that can only come from one who has allowed the Holy Spirit to heal the deepest of hurts. You opened your heart to Jesus and trusted Him with everything. He *is* worthy of that trust. Only He could transform you from the girl you once were into the lady He has called you to be. Remain close to Him as you continue walking in victory over each one of the enemies who had stolen your identity. Embrace the uniqueness of who you are, cherish your God-given friendships, and honor your commitment to purity. It is always such a delight to meet a lady—confident, certain, and deeply lovely. My dear friend, that is exactly who you are.

Know the Voice

REFLECT

- What areas do you feel you have obtained a new level of victory in? Fear, insignificance, insecurity, etc.?
- As you step into a life that has been empowered by the Holy Spirit, what do you feel you could do now that you could not do before?
- What action can you take that demonstrates your victory over fear, insignificance, or insecurity?

REMEMBER

- To walk free from fear, insignificance, and insecurity, you must remain a woman of prayer and always be dependent on the Holy Spirit.
- God is *with you*!
- "For God has re-created you all over again in His perfect righteousness, and you now belong to Him in the realm of true holiness" (Eph 4:24).

RESPOND

Father God,

Thank You for the journey I have been on with You. Thank You for revealing enemies that have taunted me for years. Most of all, thank You for the victory You won for me so that I could be free forever. There is no enemy too great for You. You have overcome them all! Let my life be a reflection of Your love and power—that every person, no matter how broken they are, can experience love that heals and transforms them. Let the beauty of Your Holy Spirit become a fountain of life that pours from my own heart into the lives around me. All of my life is Yours. Amen.

Notes

CHAPTER 4: FIND SIGNIFICANCE

1. Marianne Williamson, *A Return To Love* (New York: Harperone, 2014), 190–191.

CHAPTER 5: SILENCE INSECURITY

1. *Inside Out*, directed by Pete Docter and Ronnie Del Carmen (Emeryville, CA: Pixar Animation Studios, 2015).
2. This exercise is derived from an inner healing prayer ministry (http://bethelsozo.com).
3. Tyler Joseph and Twenty One Pilots, "Stressed Out," *Blurryface*, Fueled By Ramen, 2015. Accessed 1 Apr 2019.
4. Rodney J. Korba, "The Rate of Inner Speech," *Perceptual and Motor Skills*, vol. 71, no. 3 (Dec. 1990): 1043–1052, https://doi.org/10.2466/pms.1990.71.3.1043.

CHAPTER 6: REDEFINE BEAUTY

1. Rick Renner, *Sparkling Gems from the Greek, Vol. 1.* (Tulsa: Teach All Nations, 2003), 753–755.

CHAPTER 8: SURVIVE DATING

1. *Pride And Prejudice*, directed by Joe Wright (Working Title Films in association with Studio Canal, 2005).

2. Alan Menken et al. "When Will My Life Begin," from movie *Tangled*, Walt Disney, 2019. Accessed 1 Apr 2019.

CHAPTER 10: BE A FRIEND

1. Aimee Groth, "You're The Average Of The Five People You Spend The Most Time With," *Business Insider* (2012): https://www.businessinsider.com/jim-rohn-youre-the-average-of-the-five-people-you-spend-the-most-time-with-2012-7.

2. My sister, Lindsey Doss, has written her detailed story and her amazing miracle of restoration in a book titled *The Way Home*, which is available on Amazon.

About the Author

Lauren Bentley is a member of the leadership team at the Ramp, where she also serves as the Director of Events. Lauren is passionate to see young women overcome fear and insignificance, which led to the development of *Reinvent*, a curriculum taught in the Ramp School of Ministry. In 2014, she established Hamilton Christian Academy, the first private Christian school in her hometown of Hamilton, Alabama.

Lauren earned a Bachelor of Science degree from the University of North Alabama and graduated from the National Institute for Christian Leadership. She and her husband, Samuel, live in Hamilton with their four children: Lydia, William, Caroline, and Jonathan.

STAY CONNECTED

GOODBYE GIRL, HELLO LADY

laurenbentley.org